INJURY VICTIMS' RIGHTS TO

MAXIMUM CASH

The facts on how to collect money from insurance companies, corporations, doctors, landlords, stockbrokers, businessmen, or anyone who has caused you injury or loss.

by

James J. Shapiro

DISCLAIMER:

This publication is designed to provide general information about claims for personal and financial injuries. No lawyer should give legal advice about a specific problem or question unless he or she knows all of the facts and circumstances surrounding the case and the client. Buying or reading this book does not make you a client of the author. You become a client by making an agreement for representation with a particular lawyer. Such agreements are generally put in writing, in the form of a retainer statement that the lawyer will ask you to sign.

The laws in every state vary. Each case has different facts and circumstances. The author and publisher specifically disclaim any personal liability, loss, or risk incurred as a consequence of the use, either directly or indirectly, of any information in this book. The author and publisher are not engaged in rendering legal, accounting, insurance, or other professional services by publishing this book. If legal advice or other expert assistance is required, the services of a competent professional person should be sought.

Second Edition----1994
ISBN: 1--8835270--1--5

QUESTIONS, FREE UPDATES, AND HOW TO REACH THE AUTHOR

If you have questions about this book...

If you would like free updates to this book...

If you would like to receive a free newsletter...

Contact James Shapiro at 1-800-345-6LAW
(1-800-345-6529)

CONTENTS

SECTION ONE

INTRODUCTION

DEDICATED TO MY FATHER, SIDNEY

My father has always believed in me. He inspired me to follow in his footsteps and attend law school. Together, we formed the law firm of Shapiro and Shapiro. In March of 1986, I suggested that Shapiro & Shapiro advertise on television. Many people thought that I was too eager to develop the law practice and were against my desire to advertise. My father stood by my side. He understood that advertising would reach injured people who might not otherwise have access to a lawyer.

My father has practiced law for more than 50 years. In those 50 years, he has helped thousands of people. All of the lawyers and judges I meet praise his compassionate heart. I am fortunate to have such an amicable and respectable person as a best friend, business partner, and most importantly, as a Father.

SPECIAL DEDICATION

This book is not complete without a mention of a very special attorney, Lori Henkel. As the senior litigator at Shapiro & Shapiro, she has helped hundreds of clients to recover the cash and benefits that they truly deserve from insurance companies, corporations, and other defendants. Lori fights hard for the rights of people who have been injured. She has contributed greatly to this book and to Shapiro & Shapiro.

To Lori----never give up your drive to win, and thank you for your help with this book.

A PERSONAL INTRODUCTION FROM
JAMES J. SHAPIRO, ESQ.

My name is James Shapiro. I have helped thousands of people collect millions of dollars for their legal claims. I am proud to be known as a tough, smart lawyer who gets results.

I only represent victims of injuries----be they personal injuries or injuries of a financial nature. I never represent corporations or insurance companies. I have one goal. That goal is to help victims of personal and financial injuries collect what is fair and right.

For years, I have fought insurance companies, large corporations, and other defendants. I know that this is the only way to protect my clients' legal rights.

This book contains information about how to obtain cash and benefits if you have suffered losses due to bodily injuries, misrepresentations by stockbrokers or agents of business franchises, or discrimination by an employer or other entity.

For readers who need a lawyer, this book will describe how to hire a lawyer on a contingent fee basis----at no cost unless you win. For readers who are close to settling a claim, this book contains important questions to ask your lawyer before you settle.

I believe the greatest thing I can do as an attorney is to help victims of personal and financial injuries obtain what is just and fair.

WHAT THIS BOOK CAN DO FOR YOU

This book will answer many questions that you may have, and will tell you secrets that insurance companies, product manufacturers, stockbrokers, franchisors, and those who engage in discriminatory conduct hope you will never know:

- What to do if you are in an accident

- What to do if you believe that you have been injured due to exposure to toxic substances

- What to do if you have sustained financial losses due to investments or involvement in a franchise

- What to do if you believe that you have been the victim of discrimination

- What is medical malpractice?

- What is insurance company bad faith?

- What are "toxic torts"?

- What constitutes actionable misconduct by a stockbroker?

- How to win money even if:
  —You were at fault for an accident
  —You were aware that you were being exposed to toxic substances
  —You consented to a risky investment
  —You continued to work for an employer who engaged in discriminatory conduct

- Situations in which you should not speak to the insurance company or representatives of the other side

- How to select the best lawyer for your case

- How to determine the value of your case

- How to decide whether to go to court or settle

- Whether a lawyer can give you a cash advance

- A checklist to review before you settle any case

- Telephone numbers to complain about insurance companies, unsafe products and work conditions, unfair business practices, and discriminatory acts.

Insurance companies, product manufacturers, stockbrokers, franchisors, and employers have investigators, expert witnesses, lawyers, and lots of money. Most individuals lack such resources----and the other side knows it. This book contains information that will help you to fight back. With this information, you can collect the cash and benefits to which you are entitled!

GET ALL OF THE FACTS on how to COLLECT MONEY from INSURANCE COMPANIES, CORPORATIONS, LANDLORDS, STOCKBROKERS, DOCTORS, or ANYONE WHO HAS CAUSED YOU INJURY OR LOSS.

SECTION TWO

ACCIDENTS

INTRODUCTION

What does "personal injury" mean?

Examples of personal injuries are cuts, scars, broken bones, burns, head trauma, and paralysis. Only a person, not a piece of property, can sustain a bodily or personal injury.

Personal injuries often occur as a result of accidents. Common types of accidents that result in personal injuries include automobile collisions, incidents where individuals slip and fall, and injuries resulting from the improper design or construction of products.

If you sustain a personal injury as a result of any type of accident, you will probably have doctor bills and other medical expenses associated with your treatment. You might also lose time from work, and therefore suffer a loss of earnings. In addition, you will probably experience pain and suffering as a result of your injury. Finally, in the case of some injuries, you may be left with a permanent disability. When you bring a lawsuit, you are generally seeking to recover for these items.

Things to do after an accident:

1. Attend to your injuries.

   Call an ambulance if anyone involved in the accident has sustained serious injuries.

   Even if you think that your injuries are minor, you should see a doctor after the accident. Injuries that appear minor can sometimes be serious. Only a doctor can properly evaluate your injuries to determine the proper treatment.

A doctor's statement of your injuries is important for your claim. Insurance companies rely on documents. If you do not see a doctor within 24 hours of an accident, the insurance company could doubt the seriousness of your injury.

2. Report the accident.

For a motor vehicle accident, call the police. The responding officer will file a report that includes the date, time, location, witnesses, and a description of how and why the accident happened. You should also notify your own insurance company promptly after the accident.

If the accident happened on someone else's property, immediately notify the owner, landlord, or manager of the accident. Report as much information about the accident as you can, including exact location of the accident, and the names and addresses of all witnesses and parties involved, and obtain a copy of this report.

3. In the presence of witnesses, ask the other person about the accident.

If the other party admits that the accident was their fault, your case could be strengthened. For example, after a motor vehicle accident where the other driver failed to obey a traffic signal, ask "why didn't you stop for the red light?" If the other party admits that they were not paying attention, your chances of winning in court or negotiating a favorable settlement may be improved.

4. Consult with a lawyer.

If you have been injured in an accident, you will probably want to speak with an experienced personal injury lawyer who is backed by resources of a law firm that specializes in injury claims.

Most personal injury lawyers will not charge you a fee to discuss your case. If your case is accepted, there will usually be no legal fee unless the lawyer collects a settlement for you. Personal injury lawyers usually charge a percentage of the settlement. This fee arrangement is called a "contingent fee". The contingent fee allows victims of accidents to hire the lawyer of their choice even if they have little or no income.

If you do not contact a lawyer, you may not learn about your legal rights or the benefits that are available to you. Further, you run the risk of inadvertently making a statement to a representative of the other side that could jeopardize your claim. If you retain a lawyer, he or she will communicate with the other side on your behalf.

5. Tell your doctor and lawyer about all of your injuries.

If one part of your body is badly injured, you may forget to let your doctor know about other injuries that appear less serious. Yet sometimes these "minor" injuries may be more serious in the long run than the injuries that initially seemed the worst. You should tell your doctor about all of your injuries. You cannot recover for injuries that have not been documented by your doctor.

You should also tell your lawyer about all of your injuries. Your lawyer needs to know the full extent of your injuries to help you get the maximum amount for your claim.

Things you should not do after an accident.

1. Do not leave the scene without reporting the accident.

   Do not leave the accident scene without reporting the accident to the police, property owner, landlord, manager or some other person. To recover on your claim, you must be able to prove that the accident actually happened. If you do not report the accident, the insurance company for the other side might argue that the accident never occurred.

   If your motor vehicle or property was involved in the accident, you should report the incident to your own insurance company.

   The information that you provide when reporting the accident should be brief. Provide only the information necessary to describe how, where, and when the accident occurred.

2. Do not give statements, other than to report the accident.

   Do not make any recorded or written statements to anyone, except to report the accident as described above. The person asking for the statement could be working for the other side. Someone who is working for the other side may ask confusing questions about the accident. They may be recording the conversation. If you become confused while answering such questions, you could hurt your case.

3. Do not delay in seeking medical care.

Even if your injuries are minor, you should seek medical attention. In order to recover for your injuries, a doctor must state what injuries were caused by the accident.

4. Do not miss your medical appointments.

Missing doctor visits may create impressions such as (1) your injuries were not serious enough to justify seeing a doctor; (2) you are not making your best effort to get better; or (3) you made your injuries worse by failing to keep medical appointments. Under such circumstances, the adjuster for the other side's insurance company may believe that you do not care about your case. A person who appears not to care about their injuries may be offered less money than someone who follows all medical advice.

5. Do not sign any documents for the other side without consulting your lawyer.

If you sign a release, a settlement agreement, or a check, you will probably end your rights to make further claims against the responsible parties. You can only settle a case one time. You can not go back and ask for more, even if you are still hurt, get worse, or learn new information that strengthens your case. Never sign anything without your lawyer's advice.

6. Do not allow the other side to review your medical records without consulting your lawyer.

A large part of your claim rests on your medical condition. If you give a medical authorization to an insurance company, the insurance company can get your medical records before you ever see them. Sometimes these records contain inaccurate statements or do not include all of your injuries and complaints.

Sometimes your medical records contain information about a condition that is irrelevant to your claim. Such information could be used against you by the other side. Your lawyer should first review all medical records to determine if the other side is entitled to receive them.

7. Do not submit to a medical examination set up by the other side without consulting your lawyer.

Insurance companies spend millions of dollars each year to conduct medical examinations of people who have been injured. These examinations are performed by doctors chosen by the insurance companies. Such examinations often result in a written opinion that is not favorable for the injured person's case. You should therefore go to an examination by a doctor hired by the other side only if your lawyer advises you to attend.

8. Do not admit fault.

Even if you think you are at fault for the accident, do not make such a statement before consulting with your lawyer. If you state that you were at fault, such admission could be used in court against you.

9. Do not offer to pay for any damage caused by the accident.

Never offer to pay for damages to other people, vehicles or property. You probably have insurance. Only your insurance company should offer to pay money to others.

10. Do not withhold any information about the accident from your lawyer.

To give you the best representation, your lawyer needs to know everything about the accident. Never lie to your lawyer. Tell your lawyer everything, even facts that seem unfavorable. Your lawyer needs to know any unfavorable facts about your claim. He or she can minimize these facts while emphasizing those that support your case.

The insurance company will investigate the accident. This investigation will probably disclose any facts that are not favorable to you. If the insurance company knows about these unfavorable facts, but you have failed to mention them to your lawyer, your lawyer will be at a disadvantage. Further, your version of the accident will seem less believable, and you could receive far less money that your case might be worth.

MOTOR VEHICLE ACCIDENTS

Introduction

To recover money for pain, suffering, and permanent injuries that you have sustained as a result of a motor vehicle accident, you must be able to prove that someone other than you was negligent, or careless, and that such negligence caused you to sustain your injuries. If you are unable to prove that someone else's negligence caused your injuries, you may be unable to recover. For example, going through a red light is a negligent act. But unless an accident and injuries occur as result, the driver who ran the light could not be sued for his or her negligence.

There may also be specific requirements about what kind of injuries you must have in order to bring a case arising out of an automobile accident. Such requirements are generally governed by state law. If you have sustained injuries as a result of a motor vehicle accident, you should consult with a lawyer to learn whether your injuries are compensable.

What insurance coverages are available if you are injured in a motor vehicle accident?

1. No-fault coverage

   In most states, no-fault insurance is required on all motor vehicles (although motorcycles are frequently exempt from this requirement). No-fault insurance generally pays for an injured person's medical expenses and lost earnings due to injuries sustained in a motor vehicle accident. These payments are made to the injured person regardless of who was at fault for the accident.

No-fault insurance is separate from the insurance that may be available to compensate you for your pain, suffering and permanent injuries associated with a motor vehicle accident. The coverage that compensates you for these injuries is called liability or bodily injury coverage.

No-fault coverage is generally paid by the insurance company for the vehicle that you were in when the accident occurred. If you were a pedestrian or on a bicycle, the insurance company for the vehicle that struck you will probably pay for your no-fault benefits.

2. Bodily injury coverage

If you are injured in a motor vehicle accident that was caused by the negligence of someone other than yourself, you may be able to make a claim to recover for your pain, suffering and permanent injuries associated with the accident. The coverage that compensates you for these injuries is called liability or bodily injury coverage. This claim is separate from, and in addition to, your claim for no-fault benefits.

Bodily injury coverage comes from the insurance company for the vehicle that was at fault for the accident. Your bodily injury and no-fault claims could both be paid by the same company, if the vehicle that you were in at the time of the accident was at fault, or if you were a pedestrian or bicyclist.

When you bring a lawsuit, you are generally seeking to recover money from the bodily injury coverage applicable to the vehicle that was at fault for the accident.

How to recover even if you were at fault for an accident.

After a motor vehicle accident, the police or witnesses may say that you were at fault. You may even have been given a ticket for the accident. This does not automatically mean that you are not entitled to benefits for injuries that you sustained.

1. Medical expenses and lost earnings

   If your accident occurs in a state that requires no-fault coverage, you are entitled to collect no-fault benefits for your medical bills and for some lost wages, even if you were at fault for the accident. No-fault gets its name because the insurance company cannot consider who is at fault when paying benefits.

   In states that do not have no-fault laws, often referred to as "tort states," you can often collect money for lost wages and medical expenses even if you contributed to causing the accident. This is because in most accidents, no one person is 100% at fault.

2. Pain, suffering, and permanent injuries

   Many states have laws that allow injured people to recover for pain, suffering, and permanent injuries, even if the injured person's own negligence partially contributed to the accident. Even if your conduct contributed to the accident, you may be able to bring a lawsuit to recover for such damages—because the other party may have contributed to causing the accident as well.

   For example, if you go through a red light and are involved in an accident, you are partially at fault. But it is possible that the other driver has some responsibility as well. The other driver may have seen you going through the red light, but made no effort to avoid you. The other driver's attention may have been distracted. The other driver may have been speeding or driving while intoxicated.

For purposes of this example, assume that you were 80% responsible for the accident and the other party was 20% responsible, and that the full value of your injuries is $100,000.00. The law in some states, including New York, would allow you to recover, but would reduce the value of your injuries by 80%—the amount that you were at fault for the accident. You would therefore be entitled to recover $20,000.00.

How to recover even if you receive a ticket for an accident

If you receive a ticket as a result of a motor vehicle accident, you may feel that the ticket is proof that you were at fault. But a ticket is not proof of fault. The police officer who issued the ticket probably did not see the accident happen. The ticket is probably based upon nothing more than the officer's opinion. Only a court can decide, after evidence is presented at a trial, if a ticket is valid.

Even if the charges contained in the ticket are proved to be true, they do not mean that you are completely at fault. The other driver's conduct may have also contributed to the accident.

In some states, a ticket from an accident cannot be used as evidence against you in your personal injury case unless you plead guilty to the ticket. If you enter a plea of guilty to the ticket, however, your guilty plea could be interpreted as a statement that you caused the accident. You should therefore never enter a guilty plea to any ticket received as a result of a motor vehicle accident without consulting an attorney.

What is underinsured motorist coverage?

Automobile insurance policies have limits as to how much money will be paid to compensate an injured person. These policy limits are sometimes insufficient. The injured person has no control over the policy limits available, since these are governed by the bodily injury coverage for the other driver----the at-fault party. Protection from the potentially inadequate policy limits of other drivers is available, however, in the form of underinsured motorist coverage.

Underinsured motorist coverage is coverage that you purchase from your own automobile insurance company. If your liability policy limits are greater than those of the other driver, your underinsured motorist coverage may be available to help compensate you for your injuries.

Some states require insurance agents to tell you about the availability of underinsured motorist coverage. If you have questions about whether you presently have such coverage, you should consult your attorney or insurance agent.

Things to do if you are injured in a motor vehicle accident.
1. Immediately call an ambulance if anyone is hurt. If you are injured, go immediately to the hospital or to your doctor.

2. Call the police to report the accident.

3. Wait for a police officer to arrive before moving any vehicles, unless leaving the vehicles will create a safety hazard. If vehicles are being moved, note their position before moving them.

4. Write down the name(s) of the driver and owner of the other vehicle, and the name of their insurance company.

5. Get the name, address and phone numbers of any witnesses.

6. Ask the other driver why he or she caused the accident (for example, "Why did you run the red light?").

7. Promptly notify your own insurance company of the accident.

8. If possible, obtain photographs of the damage to all vehicles.

9. Call a lawyer who is experienced with auto accident cases.

10. Never give a statement, sign anything or admit fault without first talking to a lawyer.

SLIP AND FALL ACCIDENTS

Generally speaking, property owners are required to keep their property in a reasonably safe condition and are required to provide warnings of any unsafe conditions. Failure to maintain property in a reasonably safe condition or to provide warnings of hazards may constitute negligence. If you sustain injuries as a result of such negligence, you may be able to bring a claim against the owner of the property.

A very important fact in any slip and fall accident is whether the property owner was aware of the hazard that caused your injury **before** your accident occurred. If the owner knew or should have known of the hazard, and failed to remove it or warn you of its existence, the property owner could be liable for your injuries.

There are many hazards which might cause or contribute to a slip and fall accident. These hazards include buildups of snow and ice on outdoor sidewalks; product spills in grocery stores; slippery floors, absence of handrails on stairs, and poor lighting. Any such conditions should be pointed out to the owner of the property where the fall occurred, as well as to any witnesses to the accident.

Witness statements are particularly important in slip and fall cases, so be sure to ask the names and addresses of anyone who saw the cause of your fall, or who may have reported the hazard to the property owner **before** you were injured. In addition, you should obtain and review a copy of any written accident report, which should include a description of the hazard and the names of all witnesses.

Some property owners have insurance that will pay for some of your medical expenses associated with a slip and fall accident. There is no guarantee, however, that any of your damages will be paid without commencing a lawsuit.

CONSTRUCTION AND OTHER WORK-RELATED ACCIDENTS

While laws applicable to construction and other work-related accidents vary from state to state, many states have enacted laws that protect workers who are injured while they are on the job. Workers' compensation, which is more fully discussed in Section Fourteen, provides one example of such laws. Workers' compensation benefits insure that all workers injured during the scope of their employment will receive compensation for lost earnings, and coverage for medical expenses associated with their injuries. These benefits are paid by the insurance company for the employer of the injured person. Therefore, the law prohibits the injured person from suing the employer for his or her injuries----even if the employer is completely responsible for causing the accident that resulted in those injuries.

But what if a worker was injured:

- in a car accident while on the way from the workplace to a business meeting

- in a fall caused by a buildup of ice and snow on the sidewalk of a building where they were making a delivery for their employer

- when their foot became trapped in a defective machine

- in a fall from an elevated height while performing construction work on an office building

In each of these examples, the injured worker may be able to collect workers' compensation **and** bring a lawsuit against someone other than their employer. Such lawsuits are sometimes referred to as "third party claims," because a third party (someone other than the employer) is being sued.

When an injured worker brings a third party claim, he or she will generally be required to reimburse workers compensation from the third party settlement proceeds for all benefits that compensation has paid. This requirement that workers compensation be repaid is called a lien. Liens are more fully discussed in Section Eleven.

Individuals who work in construction trades are particularly susceptible to work-related injuries, because construction work requires extreme physical exertion and often must be performed at elevated heights. Some states, such as New York, have enacted laws that furnish special protection for workers in construction trades.

This law requires property owners and general contractors to provide safety devices to workers who perform their jobs at elevated heights. The worker need only demonstrate that he or she fell from an elevated height and was injured while performing construction or repair work on a building or structure, and that safety devices such as ropes or harnesses were not furnished. If the worker can establish these points, he or she has proved that the owner of the property and/or general contractor for the job is responsible for the injuries sustained. Even if the worker's own conduct caused or contributed to the accident, such conduct may not be held against the worker. The only issue then left to be resolved is the value of the worker's injuries.

ACCIDENTS CAUSED BY DEFECTIVE PRODUCTS

If you are injured by a defective product, you may be entitled to compensation from the product's manufacturer or seller. Products have been found defective because of the way in which they were designed or manufactured, as well as the failure to provide instructions or warnings.

Before using any product, you should always read the instructions furnished by the product's manufacturer or seller. Follow these instructions as you use the product. Do not make alterations or repairs to the product except as directed by the manufacturer and/or seller's instructions. If you do not use the product as advised by the manufacturer, the manufacturer could raise such misuse as a defense against you, thereby minimizing or destroying the value of your claim.

If you sustain an injury due to a defective product, the product should be preserved and not altered in any way. You should retain the proof of purchase and any instruction booklet or warranty information that might have been delivered with the product. It is also important to obtain the names of witnesses to the event, as well as the name of the manufacturer and/or seller of the product involved.

Cases involving product defects should be investigated as soon as possible in order to properly preserve the evidence, identify the manufacturer or the product, and determine the length of time left to bring a lawsuit.

SECTION THREE

EXPOSURE TO TOXIC SUBSTANCES

ASBESTOS

Asbestos is a fibrous mineral that can be highly toxic when inhaled, absorbed, or otherwise ingested by the body. For many years, asbestos was a commonly used insulation material. Individuals who have worked in construction trades, manufacturing plants, railroads, and other occupations where insulation or construction materials are present may have been exposed to asbestos

Asbestos fibers, when taken into the body, can cause ailments including asbestosis, mesothelioma, and a number of cancers. Ordinarily, asbestos related health problems do not develop without extended exposure, but some individuals can develop problems based on exposures that are relatively limited.

Asbestos is generally regarded as most dangerous when it is airborne. If you encounter asbestos in your home or workplace, you should not remove it yourself. Professional asbestos abatement services are available, and such agencies should be consulted to ensure that the asbestos is removed and disposed of in a safe, environmentally sound manner.

If you believe that you have been exposed to asbestos and have sustained injuries as a result of such exposure, you may wish to seek legal counsel. Thousands of individuals have already recovered monies as a result of legal actions against the manufacturers of asbestos.

A wealth of information is available showing that the manufacturers of asbestos were aware of their products' highly toxic nature, and that these manufacturers chose to ignore such evidence when placing asbestos into the marketplace. Therefore, the primary burden on an individual who has been injured by asbestos in bringing legal action is to make sure that (1) his or her claim is timely filed and not barred by any applicable statute of limitations; and (2) to identify all asbestos containing products to which he or she was exposed.

Statutes of limitation, which are discussed more fully in Section Twelve, require that most legal cases be filed within a specified time. If you fail to file a case within the time specified by law, you will receive no recovery, regardless of the severity of your injuries. Statutes of limitation with regard to asbestos claims differ from state to state. Therefore, if you believe that you have been injured due to exposure to asbestos, you should contact an attorney immediately to learn what statute of limitation applies to your case.

Individuals who have been injured by exposure to asbestos must be able to identify products to which they were exposed in order to establish their right to recover against particular asbestos manufacturers. Product identification can be accomplished in a number of ways. For example, if you consult with an attorney with regard to a potential asbestos claim, you may be asked whether you remember the names of any products that were present in your workplace. Your attorney may ask you to review a book of photographs of various asbestos products, which may refresh your memory about what products were present at your jobsite. You may also be asked if you remember the names of any co-workers, supervisors, or other personnel from the companies, unions, or worksites where you were exposed. Even if you do not recall the names of asbestos products that were present, these individuals may remember, thereby establishing a link between particular products and your injuries. Further, such individuals or entities may have records of what supplies were ordered for particular jobsites.

If you were exposed to asbestos during the course of your employment, you may also be entitled to recover workers' compensation benefits for injuries that you have sustained. Like statutes of limitation, workers' compensation laws vary from state to state. If you believe you have sustained an injury due to workplace exposure to asbestos, consultation with an attorney may assist you in clarifying your rights to recover workers' compensation, as well as other monies for your pain, suffering, and permanent injuries.

SILICONE IMPLANTS

Silicone implants have been available for over 25 years. Such implants are commonly comprised of a shell made of elasticized silicone, and a filling of silicone gel. The most widely marketed type of silicone implants are breast implants, which have been used for both cosmetic enhancement of the breasts, and for reconstruction after breast surgery.

Silicone implants have been associated with physical problems that are both localized (related to the breast only) and systemic (related to the whole body).

An implant is a foreign substance to the human body. When a foreign substance is introduced into the body, the body's normal response is to isolate that substance. This reaction results in the formation of hard capsules around the silicone implants. This hardening frequently creates an unnatural firmness to the breasts, and extreme discomfort to the implant recipient.

Many implants are susceptible to ruptures while inside of the recipient's body. When an implant ruptures, it allows silicone gel contained within the implant to escape. While such escaped silicone gel may be confined within the hard capsule that forms around the implant, it may also migrate to other parts of the body. Further, ruptures frequently cause cosmetic deformities, such as indentation or movement of the implant.

Another means by which silicone may leave the implant is through gel bleed. Gel bleed has been shown to occur with virtually all silicone implants. Gel bleed occurs when tiny beads of the silicone gel encased in the implant's silicone envelope seep out, even though there may be no distinct rupture. It is believed that after a period of time, these seepages of silicone enter the body.

Silicone is believed to create adverse effects to the immune system, thereby causing the implant recipient to experience symptoms including:

- extreme fatigue;

- joint and muscle pain;

- hair loss;

- dryness of eyes and mouth;

- numbness in extremities;

- memory loss

Silicone implants have also been associated with serious autoimmune diseases, including lupus and scleroderma. Further, silicone implants may be a factor in neurological disorders and some cancers.

Long before silicone implants were placed on the market, implant manufacturers' own research disclosed that silicone could cause serious health problems. Despite such findings, the manufacturers chose to aggressively market silicone implants to plastic surgeons and to the general public.

Silicone has also been used in a number of other medical devices. Such devices include artificial joints, dental implants, and cosmetic implants to enhance or restore the shape of other body parts. Further, silicone has been used in direct injections to enhance body parts, particularly facial features such as the cheeks and lips.

If you have been exposed to silicone or silicone implants, and believe that you have sustained injuries as a result, you may wish to consult an attorney. You may have a right to recover against the manufacturers of your implants, and in some cases, a claim for medical malpractice against the physician who performed the implant surgery.

Before meeting with the attorney, you should gather information including the name of the physician and facility where you obtained the implants, date of implant surgery, and any records that you possess pertaining to this surgery. Of particular importance is any information that identifies the manufacturer of your implants. You can also assist your attorney by preparing a list of the names and addresses of all physicians and other medical care providers with whom you have treated or consulted since obtaining your implants.

If you believe that you have been injured as a result of silicone implants, you should not delay in consulting a lawyer to learn of your legal rights to recover. Failure to bring action within the statute of limitations, a time deadline set by law, could result in the loss of any rights that you have to recover. This means that no matter how serious your injuries, you could receive no money if your case is not filed before the statute of limitations expires.

ELECTROMAGNETIC FIELDS

Research has suggested a connection between electromagnetic fields and certain cancers, particularly leukemia in children. Studies have shown that children living in close proximity to power lines can be up to ten percent (10%) more likely to develop leukemia than children who do not have such exposure.

Electromagnetic fields are created by virtually all electronic devices, but toxic exposure is primarily associated with extended exposure to power lines. Devices that emit large amounts of electromagnetic radiation have also been suspected in creating toxic exposures.

If you believe that you or your family are currently being exposed to electromagnetic fields, testing is available. Utility companies may offer to perform such testing, but such companies may wish to downplay the significance of electromagnetic field exposure. It may therefore be advisable to obtain such testing through an independent agency.

If you believe that you or a family member has been damaged by exposure to electromagnetic fields, you may wish to seek legal advice. The attorney with whom you consult may be able to assist you in obtaining the information necessary to document your claim. You may be asked many questions with regard to your family's health history, as well as questions about the health of other individuals who reside in your neighborhood. Information showing an increased incidence of cancers or other serious health problems among residents of an area located in close proximity to power lines or other sources of electromagnetic radiation, will assist the attorney in proceeding with the potential claim.

As with any legal claim, a case against a power company or other source of electromagnetic fields must be commenced within a specific amount of time. By consulting with an attorney immediately, you will learn your rights with regard to the applicable statute of limitations for your case.

LEAD

Until the early 1970's, lead was commonly used as a base for paints used in the interior and exterior of many homes. Lead has been shown to have toxic effects when taken into the body. Those most commonly affected by lead poisoning are young children, who may ingest tiny chips of lead or inhale airborne lead particles.

If you live in an older home or apartment, lead paint may be present. Common places where lead paint may be found include window frames and sills, door frames, porch floors, and walls. Merely living in an environment where lead paint has been used will not harm you. Lead is only harmful if it is ingested or inhaled. Further, amounts of lead that may not be harmful to adults may be highly toxic to children, because of their smaller body size and developing nervous systems. Likewise, pregnant women should avoid exposure to lead, as such exposure may harm the developing fetus.

Common symptoms associated with children's exposure to lead based paint include listlessness, inability to concentrate, uncontrollable behavior, learning disabilities, hyperactivity, nausea, and loss of appetite. In extreme cases, children may suffer damage to their internal organs, including the brain, as a result of exposure to lead.

Many children are routinely checked for lead in their blood when they are seen by their pediatrician. If routine testing discloses the presence of lead, treatments including hospitalization for chelation therapy, or medications administered at home may be prescribed.

In some areas, the discovery of lead in a child's system is automatically reported to the local health department. The health department will notify the owner of the property that a child living on the premises has been found to have lead in their system. An inspection of the premises will be conducted, and areas where lead hazards exist will be identified. The property owner will then be required to remove, or abate, the lead hazard before the child can resume residence.

If lead is discovered in your home, you should not seek to remove it before seeking professional advice on a safe and effective way to do so. Your local health department may be able to provide you with guidelines for removing lead based paints; trained professionals also provide lead abatement services. Prior to undertaking any lead abatement project, you should be sure that all children and pets are removed from the area, and once the removal has been completed, the area should be thoroughly cleaned to remove any excess lead dust.

You should also be aware that lead may be present in plumbing lines that supply water to some residences. If you believe that lead is present in your water supply, you should contact your local water authority, or an independent plumber for advice.

Lead may also be present in the soil surrounding your home. For this reason, it is important to supervise young children when they play outdoors, to make sure that they are not ingesting soil which may contain lead. Finally, some types of pottery-type dishes may contain lead, particularly if such pottery was manufactured outside of the United States. Before purchasing or using such dishes, you should check to make sure that there is no lead content, and if in doubt, do not use such dishes for serving food.

If you believe that your child has been exposed to lead, you should bring this fact immediately to the attention of your child's pediatrician. Should testing disclose that there is lead in the child's bloodstream, the child should immediately be removed from the environment where exposure occurred. All instructions from the pediatrician regarding the child's medical care should be precisely followed, and the child's behavioral and physical changes should be closely monitored.

To protect your child from lead before such exposure occurs, you should ask your landlord to verify in writing that there is no lead present on the property. Likewise, if you are purchasing a home, you should have an inspection performed and obtain verification that no lead hazard exists. If you observe peeling paint, paint chips, or crumbling plaster on any area of the property, you should immediately provide written notification to the landlord of the existence of this condition, and of your expectation that it be fixed as soon as possible. If the condition is not remedied, you should contact your local Department of Health and/or Building Code Enforcement Department. If you fail to provide such notification, and your child is later diagnosed with lead exposure, your failure to take action may weaken your case.

TOBACCO

In 1964, the U.S. government released findings linking tobacco with lung cancer and risks associated with other health risks. Since that time, the risks associated with smoking have gained increasing recognition. Before 1964, many tobacco companies claimed that their products could actually enhance the health of users. Once these claims regarding the health benefits of tobacco were shown to be false, some smokers and former smokers who had developed serious health problems brought legal action against tobacco companies. These cases alleged that the injured people tried cigarettes based on advertisements that touted cigarettes' health benefits, then became addicted and could not break the addiction even after the health risks were disclosed.

Such cases did not meet with success. The tobacco companies, some of the largest and most powerful corporations in the country, worked hard to defeat these claims.

Later, however, the Food and Drug Administration investigated the tobacco companies. This investigation disclosed that tobacco companies intentionally put large amounts of nicotine in cigarettes, in order to make cigarettes highly addictive. In addition, this investigation showed that the tobacco companies withheld research that showed the addictive nature of nicotine from the general public. Further, cigarette manufacturers often target their advertising at very young people in an effort to create addictions that begin early, and last long into adulthood. This information may provide the foundation upon which claims for injuries due to smoking may be brought against tobacco companies.

If you are a smoker or former smoker, you may have sustained damage due to tobacco company misrepresentations and fraud regarding the addictive nature of nicotine. If you have sustained serious injuries----such as lung cancer, em-physema, or death of a family member who smoked----you may wish to consult with an attorney to investigate the possibility of a legal claim.

Information that may assist your lawyer in evaluation your potential claim might include your reasons for starting to smoke, your age at the time you became a smoker, the amount of cigarettes that you smoke per day (and whether this amount has increased over time), the brand of cigarette that you smoke, whether you have tried to stop smoking (and with what results), and your physical problems that you associate with smoking.

Some people may believe that they understood the risks of smoking, and must therefore accept the health conse-quences. But even if some of the you understood risks associated with smoking, the manufacturers' wilful failure to disclose information about the addictive nature of their products may have prevented you from understanding all of the risks. Furthermore, the highly addictive nature of nico-tine may have kept you smoking even after you recognized that cigarettes were harming you.

You should not automatically conclude that you assumed all of the risks of your cigarette or tobacco use. Reviewing your potential claim with an attorney may help you to understand what risks you assumed, and what risks the tobacco manu-facturers intentionally kept from you.

COMPUTER KEYBOARDS

Computers and keyboards are a common feature in most work places and many homes. Yet these commonly used items may carry hidden dangers and potential for injury.

Some keyboards have been associated with repetitive stress injuries, including carpal tunnel syndrome and tendonitis. Such injuries can occur if a keyboard being used over a long term basis is not properly designed to prevent injury.

Several computer keyboard manufacturers have withheld information that would have allowed users to help avoid repetitive stress injuries The manufacturers made this information available to their own employees, but failed to disclose it to the general public, including purchasers of their products

If you have sustained a repetitive stress injury or other medical problems due to your use of a computer or keyboard, it is likely that you it is can bring a claim for workers' compensation. In addition to a workers' compensation claim, you may also be able to pursue a lawsuit against the keyboard or computer manufacturer. Consultation with an attorney may help to clarify your rights.

Information that may assist an attorney in assessing your claim includes the name of the manufacturer, model number of the keyboard that you use, length of time that you used this particular keyboard, how much training you received in use of the keyboard, whether any safety information was provided to you, how many hours of your workday were spent on the keyboard, and whether you have lost any earnings due to your injuries.

Other injuries may also be associated with poorly designed keyboards, computer stations, or work spaces. Such injuries include strain to the neck and back, and damage to vision. It has also been suggested that computers, as electronic devices that emit electromagnetic fields, may cause or contribute to certain cancers, birth defects, and other medical problems. If you have sustained such injuries due to defects in the design of a computer, keyboard, or work station, you may likewise wish to seek legal advice.

OTHER TOXIC EXPOSURES

Other products that have been shown to be toxic or otherwise dangerous include DES (a drug that was given to women in order to prevent miscarriages, which has been linked to cancer in the daughters and granddaughters of the women who took it); exposure to various chemicals; and vaccines that cause severe reactions. This list provides but a few examples of other toxic exposures. If you believe that you have sustained exposure to a toxic substance and have been injured as a result, you should not hesitate to investigate your legal rights. As previously discussed, failure to timely commence legal action may bar any right you have to recover. Further, as a practical matter, failure to document your injuries and the circumstances leading to those injuries as soon as possible after the exposure occurs, may significantly weaken your case.

SECTION FOUR

MEDICAL MALPRACTICE

Medical malpractice occurs when a doctor or other medical professional fails to conduct his or her practice in accord with reasonable care, thereby causing injury to a patient. Each aspect of this definition must be proved before a medical professional may be held liable for malpractice. For example, even if a doctor exercises reasonable care, he or she may be unable to save the life of a gravely ill or injured patient. The fact that the patient dies will not make the doctor liable for malpractice, because the doctor exercised reasonable care in treating the patient. Situations that could give rise to a medical malpractice claim, however, include:

----failure to diagnose----for example, if a patient repeatedly complains of symptoms that are commonly associated with cancer, yet the doctor fails to investigate such symptoms, and the patient later dies of cancer.

----failure to obtain informed consent----for example, if a patient is scheduled for cosmetic surgery in which one of the risks is excessive scarring, but the doctor does not explain such risk and obtain the patient's consent to that risk, and the patient is left with excessive scarring after the surgery.

----performing a surgical procedure on the wrong patient, or on the wrong part of a patient's body.

----leaving a surgical instrument inside of a patient's body.

In most medical malpractice claims, the patient's medical history and relationship with the medical professional are scrutinized by the opposing lawyer. While communications between doctors and their patients are ordinarily confidential, such confidentiality may be lifted once a lawsuit is commenced.

Proving that a medical professional has committed malpractice may be difficult. The only people qualified to determine whether malpractice has occurred are other doctors. A doctor who is called upon to testify may sympathize with the medical professional against whom the case is being brought. Such a doctor may present testimony that is unfavorable to the injured person.

No one wants to feel that they have been harmed by their doctor. You can help to avoid such feelings by selecting a doctor who regularly handles your type of medical problem. Provide the doctor an accurate and complete medical history, including information about any allergies, prior problems, current symptoms, and medications you take. Attend all exams, treatments, and referrals scheduled by your doctor. Notify your doctor immediately if you have side effects from any medicine prescribed for you, or if you get worse for any reason.

The doctor needs complete information to properly diagnose and treat you. Information that you regard as unimportant may be critical to your care. Only your doctor can decide what information is important.

If your doctor advises you to undergo surgery or if you have questions about your doctor's treatment plan for a serious condition, you may wish to seek a second opinion. Getting a second opinion is not disrespectful to your doctor. Second opinions are so important that many health insurance policies require that a second opinion be obtained before surgery is performed.

SECTION FIVE

STOCKBROKER MISCONDUCT

IS YOUR STOCKBROKER ON YOUR SIDE?

Stockbrokers are salespeople. Stockbrokers generally work for brokerage firms, which make commissions when an investor buys or sells securities. The brokerage firm pays the stockbroker a percentage of the firm's commission on the transaction. The more transactions that a particular broker handles, the more commissions that are generated for the brokerage firm and thus for the individual broker. While brokers want investors to use their services, they sometimes do not keep track of how much profit an individual investor makes.

The goals of the brokerage firm (large commissions) and the goal of the investors (income and appreciation) have little common ground. When an investment yields a large return to the investor, the broker does not earn any additional commission. The broker's earnings are based on the volume of business that he or she generates for the brokerage firm. Therefore, the broker has a disincentive for making a sale from which the investor will reap large profits.

Where the brokerage firm offers large commissions for selling particular securities, brokers have an incentive to sell those securities to investors. But ironically, payment of a large commission to the broker lowers the chance of the investor earning a profit. For example, sales of limited partnerships can earn the broker very large commissions. The broker may be pushed by the brokerage firm to sell as much of these high commission products as possible. Often these limited partnerships are very poor investments because the investor receives a low return (yield), has no liquidity, and runs a very high risk of losing the invested money.

The unlucky investor can be subjected to much worse than inflated commissions. An unethical broker may want more than a substantial commission on the investor's account. Such a broker may try to make extra commissions by violating the rules of the NASD (National Association of Securities Dealers) as follows:

1. Churning-Excessively trading an account just to earn commissions.

2. Unsuitable investments—Investing money in an investment not appropriate for the investor.

3. Unauthorized trading—Buying and selling securities without the investor's permission.

4. Promises not delivered—Making promises or telling half truths so that the investor will buy an investment that he or she would otherwise not buy.

Victims of stockbrokers' misconduct can fight back. Arbitration or litigation are methods by which investors who have lost money due to improper conduct by their brokers can seek to recover their losses. Federal and State laws prohibit brokers from misrepresenting investments, omitting important information about the risks associated with particular investments and recommending securities that are unsuitable for the investor. Other actionable complaints include unauthorized trading, excessive trading and failure to carry out an investor's orders.

WHAT IS UNSUITABILITY?

Unsuitable investments are those that are not appropriate for the investor's financial needs and circumstances.

When an investor opens an account with a stockbroker, the stockbroker asks questions about the investor's income, net worth, liquid net worth (cash available to invest), age, investment goals and occupation. The stockbroker needs this information to determine whether an investment is suitable for the investor's financial situation. Stockbrokers have an obligation to recommend only suitable investments.

For example, an eighty year old retiree should not invest all of his or her money in one limited partnership investment involving oil and gas, for a number of reasons:

1. No investor should place all of his or her money into one investment. If the investment fails, the investor has no money left.

2. A limited partnership is an investment for the future—perhaps 20 years from now. It is not suitable for an elderly investor, who will probably not live to receive his or her money back.

3. An investment in oil and gas is often a high risk investment. Older investors generally cannot afford the risk associated with such investments.

4. An elderly investor may need income to pay bills. An oil and gas investment does not have a reliable income stream.

5. Most oil and gas limited partnerships are not traded on an open market. If the investor needed money, the investment could not be sold to raise cash.

WHAT IS CHURNING?

Churning occurs when brokers encourage investors to needlessly buy and sell often, in order to generate more commissions.

Stockbrokers make money by getting a commission every time investors buy or sell securities. The more often a broker buys and sells on an investor's behalf, the more commissions the broker can earn.

It is often easy to tell that an account has been churned. If commissions paid to the broker exceed any reasonable amount of profit the investments could have made, the account has probably been oversold.

Investments are usually made for the long term. It is almost impossible for an investor to profit from frequent sales of stock, since the commissions will exceed any profit made. Only the broker comes out ahead when an account is churned.

WHY ARE SOME MUNICIPAL BONDS UNSAFE INVESTMENTS?

Brokers have convinced many investors that municipal bonds are a safe, secure and reliable investment. Brokers may assure investors that they will receive a fair return (interest) on the investment and have the security of a state or local government to pay back the bond.

However, the broker may not tell the investor that:

1. There may be a large spread between the buy price and sell price. This price difference represents the broker's commission. The commission can be between 1/2% to 4% of the total amount invested. Most investors never know the commission received by their broker on a municipal bond purchase or sale.

   Brokers often have discretion to mark-up or mark-down the bonds depending on what price they think the investor will pay (where the investor is buying bonds) or accept (where the investor is selling bonds). This discretionary mark-up or mark-down can change the amount of the broker's commission, and the amount that the investor pays for the bond or receives from the bond's sale.

2. Not all bonds are safe and secure. Municipal bonds are only as safe as the government authority that issues them. High yield bonds can be risky investments.

3. If interest rates go up, the investor may be stuck with the low paying bonds. If interest rates go down, the high rate may not be locked in. The issuer of the bond can often "call" bonds and re-borrow the money at a

lower rate. In such circumstances, the investor bears all of the risks of interest rate changes.

WHAT ARE WRAP ACCOUNTS?

Wrap accounts provide financial advice in exchange for a fixed annual fee. Investors are offered professional money management for a fraction of the investment normally required to get such expert advice. The investor is told that the brokerage firm can offer these services by pooling many small investors together. But such promises are frequently too good to be true.

Wrap accounts often come with large annual fees----sometimes up to 5% of the assets in the account. Yet the investor may be unaware of the hidden charges that are part of the wrap fee.

An investor who purchases a wrap account is paying one manager to manage the stocks and bonds in the portfolio, and a second manager----usually the brokerage firm----to manage the manager. Such management fees may be taken as a fee, or directly out of the assets of the fund.

Further, the wrap fee must cover a profit for the investor's own broker. By adding layer after layer of managers and brokers, the investor's "one-time" annual fee is so high that an unrealistic profit is needed to just break even.

Any trades that the investor executes may also carry fees, which are generally not included in the wrap fee. Most funds must execute their trades through the brokerage house that sends the business to them. This prevents the fund manager from obtaining the best price on a trade.

Brokers love to sell wrap accounts, because such accounts guarantee a commission on the investor's account for the whole year and require little to no work by the broker.

In summary, the broker may neglect to tell the wrap investor that:

1. The broker receives a large yearly payment just for selling a wrap investment;

2. The brokerage firm charges a large fee for picking out the "best" money manager;

3. The money manager also gets paid for overseeing your investment;

4. All trades may be required to be made through the brokerage firm that recommended the wrap account. No competition exists to lower the commissions or spreads. Even worse, since the money cannot be spread over many brokerage firms, the price of the investment could be severely hurt by the large size of the trade.

ARBITRATION

What is arbitration?

When an investor opens a new account at a brokerage firm, the investor must sign an agreement that governs the investor's rights in the event of a dispute with the firm. In most cases, the investor agrees that disputes will be resolved by arbitration rather than through a lawsuit in court.

Arbitration is an alternative to the courts to resolve disputes. The goal of arbitration is to resolve disputes quickly, inexpensively, and fairly.

The dispute is referred to one or more impartial persons who act as arbitrators. The arbitrators hear all of the evidence relating to the dispute, and then make a final and binding determination. Arbitration is private and informal.

The parties can agree in advance on certain arbitrators or can follow a procedure set up by an independent arbitration organization, such as the American Arbitration Association, to select the arbitrators.

After the arbitrators are selected, the parties must prepare for the arbitration hearing. All communications and preparations for the arbitration hearing are conducted through the arbitration organization. The arbitrators are not informed of the parties' positions until the actual hearing. Therefore, it is unlikely that evidence or arguments will be given to the arbitrators without the other party having an opportunity to contest the argument or evidence.

The parties are responsible for assembling all documents and papers needed for the hearing. As part of this preparation, the investor can request documents from the stockbroker or brokerage firm. The investor should also obtain interviews of all of the witnesses before the arbitration. Parties can subpoena documents or witnesses. The parties should make sure arrangements are made to record the arbitration.

Each party has the right to be represented by a lawyer at the hearing. Each party can present their case to the arbitrators. In most claims, the party bringing the claim presents their side first. The legal procedures followed at arbitration hearings are similar to those used in court trials. The rules of evidence are not as strictly followed at arbitration as at trial.

Most arbitration hearings proceed in the following order:

First, there is a brief opening statement by each party. Next, the claimant tells the arbitrators the remedy sought. The claimant must explain how the remedy sought is within the arbitrators' authority. Next, the witnesses testify. Cross-examination is allowed. Finally, a closing statement is given by each party.

After both sides have presented their arguments, the arbitrators declare the hearing closed. In most cases, the arbitrators have 30 days to render a decision. A decision is called an "award" in arbitration. Most awards are binding on the parties and can not be appealed. The awards are usually enforceable in the civil courts, if not complied with by the parties.

Most arbitrations for securities claims must be heard by an association specified in the investor's agreement with brokerage firm. Most agreements require binding arbitration by the National Association of Securities Dealers (NASD) or the American Arbitration Association (AAA).

The main office of the NASD is 1735 K Street NW, Washington, DC 20006. Their phone number is (202) 728--8000. The NASD rules of arbitration are found in the NASD manual. Their rules for arbitration that they call the "Code of Arbitration Procedure" is found in Chapter 3701 through Chapter 3746 of the manual.

The American Arbitration Association has its main office at 1450 West 51st Street, New York, NY 10020. The AAA has 35 offices in major cities. The rules and procedures can be received by contacting the AAA at the above address.

What are the costs of arbitration?

The cost of going to arbitration can be high, sometimes exceeding $10,000.00. Arbitration costs can include attorney fees, expert witness fees, arbitrator fees, transcript costs and fees to the arbitration association responsible for the claim. Most of these costs must be paid in advance. Most of these costs must be paid even if the investor does not recover his or her losses. The costs are as follows:

1. Claim filing fee—This fee must be paid for filing the claim with the arbitration association. For example, the NASD charges $150.00 for disputes dealing with amounts up to $50,000.00 and $250.00 for disputes dealing with amounts up to $500,000.00 dispute. This charge is non-refundable and must be paid in advance.

2. Hearing session deposit—At the time of filing a claim, the NASD also requires a hearing session deposit. A hearing session is any meeting between the parties and the arbitrators. For a three arbitrator, $50,000.00 claim, the hearing deposit is $600.00. For a $500,000.00 claim, the deposit is $1,000.00.

3. Expert witness fee—Most cases require the use of an expert witness to prove investors' losses. Expert witnesses often charge between $2,000.00 and $8,000.00 depending on the complexity of the case and the time required to testify.

Securities lawyers can charge between $100.00 and $400.00 per hour. Securities cases often require extensive legal work. This could result in thousands of dollars of legal fees.

Some lawyers handle securities cases on a contingency fee basis, and will advance the costs associated with arbitration. An attorney who represents investors on a contingency fee basis will charge no fee unless money is recovered on the investor's behalf. The lawyer will take a percentage of any recovery as their fee. Naturally, a lawyer will not agree to these terms unless they are confident in the investor's case.

Should you go to arbitration or settle?

The brokerage firm may make an offer to settle without going to arbitration. The investor will then need to decide whether to accept the settlement offer or wait for a hearing.

The advantages of settling your claim include the following:
1. You know how much you will receive.

2. You will receive your money now rather than later.

3. You have no risk of losing and getting nothing for your claim.

4. You will not have to pay additional hearing costs and expert witness fees.

5. You will not be surprised by new information that could hurt or ruin your claim.

6. You can put the matter behind you and go on with your life.

7. You will not risk the chance that the broker or brokerage firm will run out of assets or declare bankruptcy before you win. It is useless to win if you cannot collect.

The disadvantages of settling your case include the following:

1. A settlement is final. You cannot re-open the case if new information is discovered.

2. The arbitrators could give much more money than the current settlement offer.

Many claims settle before arbitration. This is because the brokerage firms and claimants both know that arbitrators can give a large award, a small award, or no award at all. Arbitration can be expensive for both sides. A lawyer's time in court is worth thousands of dollars each day. Expert witnesses' fees can be immense. The total cost of going to arbitration, combined with the unknown outcome, often makes the decision easy.

In some cases, however, the offer made by the brokerage firm is not fair. Going to arbitration may be advantageous in these instances. A small offer means little risk if the case is submitted to arbitration.

You should consult with your lawyer and ask his or her advice on settling any claim. Law firms that handle securities claims will know the brokerage firm's tactics and will know whether a settlement offer is fair. Your lawyer will also be aware of the strengths and weaknesses of your case and will be able to advise you about the risks and benefits associated with settlement and arbitration.

You can win in arbitration even if you were at fault for the loss.

After you lose money in an investment, your friends and family may tell you that it was your own fault. You might think that you knew the risks of the investment and just had bad luck or made a poor investment decision.

You can make a claim against your broker and brokerage firm even if you think you knew and took the risks in the following situations:

1. The broker lied to you about the real risks.

2. The investment was unsuitable for your investment situation or stated goals.

3. The broker made untrue promises or misrepresented the investment.

4. The broker "churned" the account by encouraging you to frequently to buy and sell securities.

5. Too much of your investment portfolio was invested in one or two risky investments.

Investors who have sustained losses often think that they are responsible for such losses. Some investors may believe that their own greed caused the loss. Such investors should consider whether the broker created the greed by making promises of a substantial profit within a short amount of time.. If the broker made unrealistic promises in order to sell the investment, the broker's conduct may be actionable, notwithstanding the investor's desire for a large, fast profit. Only a lawyer experienced in securities litigation should determine if the loss was your fault or the broker's.

HOW TO USE INFORMATION ON YOUR BROKER-AGE FORM TO SUPPORT YOUR CLAIM

When an investor opens a new account at a stock brokerage firm, he or she provides important information to the stockbroker. This information includes details about the investor's net worth, income, cash available to invest, investment goals, property ownership, age and marital status. The answers to these questions are very important, because they inform the broker of the risks that the investor can or cannot take.

In most cases investors learn about investments from their brokers. Since brokers are professionals, it is not unusual for investors to follow their broker's advice.

If a broker sells an investment that is not suitable for an investor's financial situation, the account form is the proof that the broker knew about the investor's finances. For example, a $30,000.00 investment in a risky limited partnership or in options might be an acceptable risk for a young doctor earning $350,000.00 per year, and having a liquid net worth of more than $1,000,000.00. This example assumes the doctor understands the risk.However, a similar $30,000.00 investment for a retired widow, living on Social Security with only a $50,000.00 net worth is not proper.

QUESTIONS YOUR LAWYER WILL ASK

When you first meet with your lawyer, you will be asked many questions. These questions are aimed at getting the information needed to investigate and prepare your claim. Your attorney cannot afford to be surprised later about an important piece of information. The following is a list of common questions asked by lawyers of their clients:

1. Name

2. Home address

3. Phone numbers at home and work

4. Age

5. Social Security Number

6. Marital Status

7. Spouse's name

8. Age of spouse

9. Children's names and ages

10. Occupation

11. List of all persons living in the household, their ages and if they are dependent on you

12. Name of any broker or brokerage firm to which you have made any complaints in writing or on the phone

13. Copies of any account documents you have

14. Copies of all documents received from the broker

15. Your net worth

16. Income received from the investment

17. Amount you invested with the broker, dates invested, and what types of investments made

18. Other investments that you have made and their results

19. Other brokers and brokerage firms with whom you have had accounts

20. Source of all income and amounts

21. Amount you lost

22. What was your financial situation when you made the investment(s)

23. What education and experience do you have with investing.

Your lawyer will probably ask more questions depending upon your specific case.

QUESTIONS TO ASK YOUR BROKER BEFORE YOU MAKE ANY INVESTMENT

It is important to learn about any investment before making a purchase. The following are typical questions that your broker should be able to answer:

1. How much of your money is actually going into the investment? How much of your initial investment goes for commissions, markups of the securities, expenses of the offer, and other related expenses?

2. How much is charged each year by the managers of the investment to manage your money?

3. How much are you charged by the owners or partners to oversee the managers each year?

4. What kind of market exists to sell your investment? Unless a large exchange exists to list and sell your investment you may suffer a large loss if you want to sell out.

5. How is the return of your investment guaranteed?

6. Is this investment suitable for someone your age, with your income, with your net worth, and with your investment goals?

7. What are the risks of this type of investment?

8. What are the tax aspects of your investment?

9. What prior track record exists for the same type of investment?

10. What rate of return can you expect on your money?

11. When can you expect to receive back your investment and from what source?

12. Are there any documents that you can read from the seller or sponsor of the investment?

13. Are there any published articles or other information available about the investment from sources other than the investment's sponsor?

14. Can you afford to lose the money you are investing?

15. Do you need the money for an emergency or unexpected expense in the near future?

16. Are you well diversified into different low risk investments?

Always ask your broker to put answers to your questions in writing. Then you will have proof of your broker's claims and promises.

IMPORTANT NAMES, ADDRESSES, AND PHONE NUMBERS

Most arbitrations are with the NASD or American Arbitration Association. Their main offices are listed below:

NASD (National Association of Securities Dealers)
1735 K Street NW
Washington, DC 20006
Telephone No.: 202-728-8000

American Arbitration Association
140 West 51st St
New York, NY 10020
Telephone No.: 212-484-4000
Facsimile No.: 212-765-4874

New York Stock Exchange, Inc.
Constitution and Rules can be purchased from:
Commerce Clearing House, Inc.
4025 West Peterson Ave
Chicago, Illinois 60646
Phone No.: 1-800-248-3248

Arbitration Journal
Published quarterly by American Arbitration Association
Subscriptions write to:
Hilda Melendez
American Arbitration Association
140 West 51st St
New York, NY 10020

Arbitration Times
Also published by American Arbitration Association
See address above or call 1-212-484-4000

New York Stock Exchange
11 Wall St.
New York, NY 10005

SECURITIES ARBITRATION RULES OF THE AMERICAN ARBITRATION ASSOCIATION

AS AMENDED AND EFFECTIVE ON MAY 1, 1993.

Introduction

Each year, millions of transactions involving security and commodity futures take place. Occasionally, disagreements develop over these transactions. Many of these disputes are resolved by arbitration, the voluntary submission of a dispute to a disinterested person or persons for final and binding determination. Arbitration has proven to be an effective way to resolve these disputes privately, promptly and economically.

The American Arbitration Association (AAA) is a public-service, not-for-profit organization offering a broad range of dispute-resolution services to business executives, attorneys, individuals, trade associations, unions, management, consumers, families, communities and all levels of government. Services are available through AAA headquarters in New York City and through offices located in major cities throughout the United States. Hearings may be held at locations convenient for the parties and are not limited to cities with AAA offices. In addition, the AAA serves as a center for education and training, issues specialized publications, and conducts research on all forms of out-of-court dispute settlement.

In October of 1991, the American Arbitration Association created a Securities Arbitration Task Force, comprised of representatives of various brokerage firms, customers' attorneys and others with considerable knowledge and experience in securities matters and the arbitration process. The mission of the Task Force was to consider improvements in the AAA's Securities Arbitration Rules and administrative procedures and policies that would make AAA-administered arbitration more attractive to all participants in the process. An effort was made at the same time to consider changes that would make the Securities Arbitration Rules applicable to commodity futures matters. The task force met 11 times from November 1991 through February 1993.

The report of the task force was endorsed by the AAA's Practice Committee and the rules are amended effective May 1, 1993 in response to the report.

An expedited system has been included in the rules for cases in which each party's claims involve less than $25,000, exclusive of interest and arbitration costs. This will assist parties in resolving such claims.

The rules contain procedures for the selection of arbitrators with appropriate expertise, including both those affiliated with the securities industry and those who are not. In the interest of fairness, the AAA has developed specific guidelines defining what constitutes an industry-affiliated arbitrator. Under these rules, lists of arbitrators and biographical information on each are sent to the parties for selection of the arbitrators. In addition, the arbitrators sign an oath of office and are required to disclose any relationship with the parties or their representative even if such circumstances become known after the heating commences.

These features, as well as others contained in the rules, will assist the parties in resolving disputes fairly and promptly.

Governmental agencies have issued guidelines and regulations governing arbitration of future disputes involving securities. Consistent with such regulations, the parties can provide for the arbitration of future disputes by inserting the following clause into their contracts.

Standard Arbitration Clause

Any controversy or claim arising out of or relating to this contract, or the breach thereof, shall be settled by arbitration administered by the American Arbitration Association under its Securities Arbitration Rules, and judgment on the award rendered by the arbitrator(s) may be entered in any court having jurisdiction thereof.

Arbitration of existing disputes may be accomplished by use of the following:

We, the undersigned parties, hereby agree to submit to arbitration administered by the American Arbitration Association under its Securities Arbitration Rules the following controversy: (cite briefly). We further agree that the above controversy be submitted to (one)(three) arbitrator(s). We further agree that we will faithfully observe this agreement and the rules, that we will abide by and perform any award rendered by the arbitrator(s), and that a judgment of the court having jurisdiction may be entered on the award.

The services of the AAA are generally concluded with the transmittal of the award. Although there is voluntary compliance with the majority of awards, judgment on the award can be entered in a court having appropriate jurisdiction if necessary.

Administrative Fees

The AAA's administrative fees are based on service charges. There is a filing fee based on the amount of the claim or counterclaim, ranging from $300 on claims below $25,000 to a maximum of $4,000 for claims in excess of $5 million. In addition, there are service charges for hearings held and postponements and a processing fee for prolonged cases. This fee information allows the parties to exercise control over their administrative fees. The fees cover AAA administrative services; they do not cover arbitrator compensation or expenses, reporting services, or any post award charge incurred by the parties in enforcing the award.

Mediation

The parties may wish to submit their dispute to mediation prior to arbitration. In mediation, the neutral mediator assists the parties in reaching a settlement, but does not have the authority to make a binding decision or award. Mediation is administered by the AAA in accordance with its Commercial Mediation Rules. There is no additional administrative fee where parties to a pending arbitration attempt to mediate their dispute under the AAA's auspices.

If the parties want to adopt mediation as a part of their contractual dispute settlement procedure, they can insert the following mediation clause into their contract in conjunction with a standard arbitration provision.

If a dispute arises out of or relates to this contract, or the breach thereof and if the dispute cannot be settled through negotiation, the parties agree first to try in good faith to settle the dispute by mediation administered by the American Arbitration Association and its Commercial Mediation Rules before resorting to arbitration, litigation, or some other dispute resolution procedure.

If the parties want to use a mediator to resolve an existing dispute, they can enter into the following submission.

The parties hereby submit the following dispute to mediation administered by the American Arbitration Association under its Commercial Mediation Rules (the clause may also provide for the qualifications of the mediator(s), the method of payment, the locale of meetings and any other item of concern to the parties).

Even if your contract does not provide for administration by the AAA, arbitration or mediation might be available through pilot projects involving various brokerage firms and securities exchanges. Your local AAA office can provide more information about these programs.

Large Case Procedures

Recognizing that large, complex arbitrations often present unique procedural problems, the AAA, working with attorneys, arbitrators and industry advisory groups, has developed special Supplementary Procedures for Large, Complex Disputes as part of its Large, Complex Case Dispute Resolution Program. The overall purpose of these procedures is to provide for the efficient, economical and speedy resolution of larger disputes (i.e., cases involving claims in excess of $1,000,000). Cases are administered by senior AAA staff. The procedures provide for an early administrative conference with the AAA and a preliminary hearing with the arbitrators. Documentary exchanges and other essential exchanges of information are facilitated. The procedures also provide that a statement of reasons may accompany the award, if requested by the parties. The procedures are meant to supplement applicable rules that the parties have agreed to use. They include the possibility of the use of mediation to resolve some or all issues at an early stage.

The procedures are party driven. They will apply only where the parties agree to their use (unless a court or another entity directs their application) and the parties are free to modify any provision of the procedures. Indeed, the entire process may be tailored to suit the particular requirements of the parties to any single dispute.

Securities Arbitration Rules

1. Agreement of Parties

The parties shall be deemed to have made these rules a part of their arbitration agreement whenever they have provided for arbitration by the American Arbitration Association (hereinafter AAA) or under its Securities Arbitration Rules. These rules and any amendment of them shall apply in the form obtaining at the time the demand for arbitration or submission agreement involving a securities or commodity futures dispute is received by the AAA.

2. Name of Tribunal

Any tribunal constituted by the parties for the settlement of their dispute under these rules shall be called the Securities Arbitration Tribunal.

3. Administrator and Delegation of Duties

When parties agree to arbitrate under these rules, or when they provide for arbitration by the AAA and an arbitration is initiated under these rules, they thereby authorize the AAA to administer the arbitration. The authority and duties of the AAA are established in the agreement of the parties and in these rules, and may be carried out through such of the AAA's representatives as it may direct. The AAA may, in its discretion, assign the administration of an arbitration to any of its regional offices.

4. National Panel of Arbitrators

The AAA shall establish and maintain a National Panel of Securities Arbitrators and shall appoint arbitrators as provided in these rules.

5. Initiation under an Arbitration
   Provision in a Contract

Arbitration under an arbitration provision in a contract shall be initiated in the following manner:

(a) The initiating party (hereinafter claimant) shall, within the time period, if any, specified in the contract(s), give written notice to the other party (hereinafter respondent) of its intention to arbitrate (demand), which notice shall contain a statement setting forth the nature of the dispute, the amount involved, if any, the remedy sought, and the hearing locale requested, and

(b) shall file at any regional office of the AAA three copies of the notice and three copies of the arbitration provisions of the contract, together with the appropriate filing fee as provided in the schedule. The AAA shall give notice of such filing to the respondent or respondents.

6. Answers and Third-Party Claims

A respondent may file an answering statement in duplicate with the AAA within 20 days from the commencement of administration, simultaneously sending a copy of the answering statement to the claimant. A party may also file an answer to a changed or new claim, as provided in Section 8. If no answering statement is filed within the time period stated above, it will be treated as a general denial of the claim.

83

If a counterclaim is asserted, it shall contain a statement setting forth the nature of the counterclaim, the amount involved, if any, and the remedy sought. If a counterclaim is made, the appropriate fee provided in the schedule shall be forwarded to the AAA with the answering statement.

If a respondent fails to file an answering statement within the time period stated above, the claimant may serve respondent with a written request for an answering statement. A respondent who fails to file an answer within 10 days of such a request may, in the discretion of the arbitrator, be barred from presenting any matter, argument or defense (other than a general denial) that could have been raised in an answering statement, but an arbitrator may not enter an award against a party without hearing evidence to support the making of an award. Arbitrators should endeavor to rule on requests to bar such matters prior to the hearing.

The demand or answer may assert a third-party claim against another party, if the third party is obliged to arbitrate the subject of that party's claim under these rules. The arbitrator is authorized to resolve any dispute over such joinder.

7. Initiation under a Submission

Parties to any existing dispute may start an arbitration under these rules by filing at any regional office of the AAA three copies of a written submission to arbitrate under these rules, signed by the parties. It shall contain a statement of the matter in dispute, the amount involved, if any, the remedy sought, and the hearing locale requested, together with the appropriate filing fee.

8. Changes of Claim

After filing of a claim, if either party desires to make any new or different claim or counterclaim, it shall be made in writing and filed with the AAA. Simultaneously, a copy must be sent to the other party, who shall have a period of 10 days from the date of such transmittal within which to file an answer with the AAA. After the arbitrator is appointed, however, no new or different claim may be submitted except with the arbitrator's consent.

9. Applicable Procedures

Unless the AAA in its discretion determines otherwise, the Expedited Procedures shall be applied in any case where no disclosed claim or counterclaim exceeds $25,000, exclusive of interest and arbitration costs. Parties may also agree to use the Expedited Procedures in cases involving claims in excess of $25,000. The Expedited Procedures shall be applied as described in Sections 51 through 55 of these rules, in addition to any other portion of these rules that is not in conflict with the Expedited Procedures.

All other cases shall be administered in accordance with Sections 1 through 50 of these rules.

10. Administrative Conference, Preliminary
Hearing and Mediation Conference

At the request of any party or at the discretion of the AAA, an administrative conference with the AAA and the parties and/or their representatives will be scheduled in appropriate cases to expedite the arbitration proceedings. There is no administrative fee for this service.

At the request of any party or at the discretion of the arbitrator or the AAA, a preliminary hearing with the parties and/or their representatives and the arbitrator may be scheduled by the arbitrator to specify issues to be resolved, to stipulate to uncontested facts, to schedule hearings to resolve the dispute, and to consider other matters that will expedite the arbitration proceedings. There is no administrative fee for the first preliminary hearing.

Unless the parties agree otherwise, the AAA at any stage of the proceeding may arrange a mediation conference under the Commercial Mediation Rules, in order to facilitate settlement. The mediator shall not be an arbitrator appointed to the case. Where the parties to a pending arbitration agree to mediate under the AAA's rules, no additional administrative fee is required to initiate the mediation.

11. Exchange of Information

Consistent with the expedited nature of arbitration, the arbitrator may establish (i) the extent of and schedule for production of documents and other information and (ii) identification of witnesses to be called. The arbitrator is authorized to resolve any dispute over this information exchange.

12. Fixing of Locale

The parties may agree on the locale where the arbitration is to be held. If any party requests that the hearing be held in a specific locale and the other party files no objection thereto within 20 days after notice of the request has been sent to it by the AAA, the locale shall be the one requested. If a party objects to the locale requested by the other party the AAA shall have the power to determine the locale and its decision shall be final and binding.

13. Qualifications of an Arbitrator

Any neutral arbitrator appointed pursuant to Section 14, 15, 16 or 52, or selected by mutual choice of the parties or their appointees, shall be subject to disqualification for the reasons specified in Section 20. If the parties agree in writing, the arbitrator shall not be subject to disqualification for those reasons.

Unless the parties agree otherwise, an arbitrator selected unilaterally by one party is a party-appointed arbitrator and is not subject to disqualification pursuant to Section 20.

The term "arbitrator" in these rules refers to the arbitration panel, whether composed of one or more arbitrators and whether the arbitrators are neutral or party appointed. An affiliated arbitrator is provided in Sections 14 and 18 is one who has or has had direct involvement in or relationship with the securities brokerage industry for a minimum of three years if now employed in that industry or for a minimum of five years if no longer so employed. Involvement in or relationship with would include (a) employment at a brokerage firm in a professional capacity, whether employed in sales, management, support or trading, or (b) employment as counsel, accountant or other professional who devotes a majority of his or her efforts to brokerage or brokerage-related matters. Persons out of the industry for more than 10 years are not affiliated. Persons whose firms or direct family members derive significant income from securities brokerage or brokerage-related matters, but who do not qualify as affiliated arbitrators as defined above, may not serve as arbitrators.

14. Appointment from Panel

If the parties have not appointed an arbitrator and have not provided any other method of appointment, the arbitrator shall be appointed in the following manner: immediately after the filing of the demand or submission, the AAA shall send simultaneously to each party to the dispute two lists of names and biographical information of persons chosen from the panel. The first list, from which one arbitrator will be appointed, will contain names of arbitrators affiliated with the securities industry. The second list, from which two arbitrators will be appointed, will contain names of arbitrators not affiliated with the securities industry. Additional biographical information on proposed arbitrators may be available from the AAA and will be furnished to a party upon request.

Each party to the dispute has 20 days from the transmittal date in which to strike any names objected to, number the remaining names in order of preference, and return the list to the AAA. If a party does not return the list within the time specified, all persons shall be deemed acceptable. From among the persons who have been approved on both lists and in accordance with the designated order of mutual preference, the AAA shall invite the arbitrator(s) who will serve.

If appointments cannot be made from the submitted list, the AAA will submit to the parties a final list of proposed arbitrators, consisting of a limited number of names. Each separately appearing party may strike on a peremptory basis one name for each arbitrator to be appointed, and return the list to the AAA within 10 days from the date of the AAA's transmittal to the parties. The AAA shall make the appointment(s) from the name(s) remaining on the list.

15. Direct Appointment by a Party

If the agreement of the parties names an arbitrator or specifies a method of appointing an arbitrator, that designation or method shall be followed. The notice of appointment, with the name and address of the arbitrator, shall be filed with the AAA by the appointing party. Upon the request of any appointing party the AAA shall submit a list of members of the panel from which the party may, if it so desires, make the appointment.

If the agreement specifies a period of time within which an arbitrator shall be appointed and any party fails to make the appointment within that period, the AAA shall make the appointment.

If no period of time is specified in the agreement, the AAA shall notify the party to make the appointment. If, within 20 days, an arbitrator has not been appointed by a party within the specified period, the AAA shall make the appointment.

16. Appointment of Neutral Arbitrator by Party-Appointed Arbitrators or Parties

If the parties have selected party-appointed arbitrators, or if such arbitrators have been appointed as provided in Section 15, and the parties have authorized them to appoint a neutral arbitrator within a specified time and no appointment is made within that time or any agreed extension, the AAA may appoint a neutral arbitrator, who shall act as chairperson.

If no period of time is specified for appointment of the neutral arbitrator and the party-appointed arbitrators or the parties do not make the appointment within 10 days from the date of the appointment of the last party-appointed arbitrator, the AAA may appoint the neutral arbitrator, who shall act as chairperson.

If the parties have agreed that their party-appointed arbitrators shall appoint the neutral arbitrator from the panel, the AAA shall furnish to the party-appointed arbitrators a list selected from the panel, and the appointment of the neutral arbitrator shall be made as provided in Section 14.

17. Nationality of Arbitrator in International Arbitration

Where the parties are nationals or residents of different countries, any neutral arbitrator shall, upon the request of any party, be appointed from among the nationals of a country other than that of any of the parties. The request must be made prior to the time set for the appointment of the arbitrator as agreed by the parties or set by these rules.

18. Number of Arbitrators

Where the claim of any party exceeds $25,000, the dispute shall be heard and determined by three arbitrators. Unless the parties otherwise agree, the majority shall be arbitrators not affiliated with the securities industry. All other disputes shall be heard and determined by one arbitrator not affiliated with the securities industry, as provided in Section 52.

19. Notice to Arbitrator of Appointment

Notice of the appointment of the neutral arbitrator, whether appointed by agreement of the parties or by the AAA, shall be sent to the arbitrator by the AAA, together with a copy of these rules. The signed acceptance of the arbitrator shall be filed with the AAA prior to the opening of the first hearing.

20. Disclosure and Challenge Procedure

Any person appointed as neutral arbitrator shall disclose to the AAA any circumstance likely to affect impartiality, including any bias or any financial or personal interest in the result of the arbitration or any past or present relationship with the parties or their representatives. Upon receipt of such information from the arbitrator or another source, the AAA shall communicate the information to the parties and, if it deems it appropriate to do so, to the arbitrator and others. Upon objection of a party to the continued service of a neutral arbitrator, the AAA shall determine whether the arbitrator should be disqualified and shall inform the parties of its decision, which shall be conclusive.

21. Vacancies

If for any reason an arbitrator is unable to perform the duties of the office, the AAA may, on proof satisfactory to it, declare the office vacant. Vacancies shall be filled in accordance with the applicable provisions of these rules.

In the event of a vacancy in a panel of arbitrators after the hearings have commenced, unless the parties agree otherwise, the vacancy shall be filled as provided above, and the newly constituted panel shall determine whether all or part of any prior hearing shall be repeated.

22. Date, Time and Place of Hearing

The arbitrator shall set the date, time and place for each hearing. The AAA shall send a notice of hearing to the parties at least 10 days in advance of the hearing date, unless otherwise agreed by the parties.

23. Representation

Any party may be represented by counsel or other authorized representative. A party intending to be represented shall notify the other party and the AAA of the name, address and telephone number of the representative at least three days prior to the date set for the hearing at which that person is first to appear. When a representative initiates an arbitration or responds for a party, notice of representation is deemed to have been given.

24. Stenographic Record

Any party desiring a stenographic record shall make arrangements directly with a stenographer and shall notify the other parties of these arrangements in advance of the hearing. The requesting party or parties shall pay the cost of the record, if the transcript is agreed by the parties to be, or determined by the arbitrator to be, the official record of the proceeding, it must be made available to the arbitrator and to the other parties for inspection, at a date, time and place determined by the arbitrator.

25. Interpreters

Any party wishing an interpreter shall make all arrangements directly with the interpreter and shall assume the costs of the service.

26. Attendance at Hearings; Experts

The arbitrator shall maintain the privacy of the hearings unless the law provides to the contrary. Any person having a direct interest in the arbitration is entitled to attend hearings. Although expert witnesses are generally permitted to attend the hearing, the arbitrator shall have the power to require the exclusion of any witness, other than a party or other essential person, during the testimony of any other witness. It shall be discretionary with the arbitrator to determine the propriety of the attendance of any other person.

27. Postponements

The arbitrator for good cause shown may postpone any hearing upon the request of a party or upon the arbitrator's own initiative, and shall grant a postponement when all of the parties agree.

28. Oaths

Before proceeding with the first hearing, each arbitrator may take an oath of office and, if required by law, shall do so. The arbitrator may require witnesses to testify under oath administered by any duly qualified person and, if it is required by law or requested by any party, shall do so.

29. Majority Decision

All decisions of the arbitrators must be by a majority. The award must also be made by a majority unless the concurrence of all is expressly required by the arbitration agreement or by law.

30. Order of Proceedings and Communication with Arbitrator

A hearing shall be opened by the filing of the oath of the arbitrator, where required; by the recording of the date, time and place of the hearing, and the presence of the arbitrator, the parties and their representatives, if any; and by the receipt by the arbitrator of the statement of the claim and the answering statement, if any.

The arbitrator may, at the beginning of the hearing, ask for statements clarifying the issues involved. In some cases, part or all of the above will have been accomplished at the preliminary hearing conducted by the arbitrator pursuant to Section 10.

The complaining party shall then present evidence to support its claim. The defending party shall then present evidence supporting its defense. Witnesses for each party shall submit to questions or other examination. The arbitrator has the discretion to vary this procedure but shall afford a full and equal opportunity to all parties for the presentation of any material and relevant evidence.

Exhibits, when offered by either party, may be received in evidence by the arbitrator.

The names and addresses of all witnesses and a description of the exhibits in the order received shall be made a part of the record.

There shall be no direct communication between the parties and a neutral arbitrator other than at oral hearing, unless the parties and the arbitrator agree otherwise. Any other oral or written communication from the parties to the neutral arbitrator shall be directed to the AAA for transmittal to the arbitrator.

31. Arbitration in the Absence of a Party or Representative

Unless the law provides to the contrary, the arbitration may proceed in the absence of any party or representative who, after due notice, fails to be present or fails to obtain a postponement. An award shall not be made solely on the default of a party. The arbitrator shall require the party who is present to submit such evidence as the arbitrator may require for the making of an award.

32. Evidence

The parties may offer evidence that is relevant and material to the dispute, and shall produce such evidence as the arbitrator deems necessary to an understanding and determination of the dispute. An arbitrator or other person authorized by law to subpoena witnesses or documents may do so upon the request of any party or independently.

The arbitrator shall be the judge of the relevance and materiality of the evidence offered, and conformity to legal rules of evidence shall not be necessary. All evidence shall be taken in the presence of all of the arbitrators and all of the parties, except where any of the parties is absent in default or has waived the right to be present.

33. Evidence by Affidavit and Post hearing Filing of Documents or Other Evidence

The arbitrator may receive and consider the evidence of witnesses by affidavit, but shall give it only such weight as the arbitrator deems it entitled to after consideration of any objection made to its admission.

If the parties agree or the arbitrator directs that documents or other evidence be submitted to the arbitrator after the hearing, the documents or other evidence shall be filed with the AAA for transmission to the arbitrator. All parties shall be afforded an opportunity to examine such documents or other evidence.

34. Inspection or Investigation

An arbitrator finding it necessary to make an inspection or investigation in connection with the arbitration shall direct the AAA to so advise the parties. The arbitrator shall set the date and time and the AAA shall notify the parties. Any party who so desires may be present at such an inspection or investigation. In the event that one or all parties are not present at the inspection or investigation, the arbitrator shall make a verbal or written report to the parties and afford them an opportunity to comment.

35. Interim Measures

The arbitrator may direct whatever interim measures are deemed necessary with respect to the dispute, including measures for the conservation of property, without prejudice to the rights of the parties or to the final determination of the dispute. Such interim measures may be taken in the form of an interim award and the arbitrator may require security for the costs of such measures.

36. Closing of Hearing

The arbitrator shall specifically inquire of all parties whether they have any further proofs to offer or witnesses to be heard. Upon receiving negative replies or if satisfied that the record is complete, the arbitrator shall declare the hearing closed.

If briefs are to be filed, the hearing shall be declared closed as of the final date set by the arbitrator for the receipt of briefs. If documents are to be filed as provided in Section 33 and the date set for their receipt is later than that set for the receipt of briefs, the later date shall be the date of closing the hearing. The time limit within which the arbitrator shall endeavor to make the award shall start to run, in the absence of other agreements by the parties, upon the closing of the hearing.

37. Reopening of Hearing

The hearing may be reopened on the arbitrator's initiative, or upon application of a party, at any time before the award is made. If reopening the hearing would prevent the making of the award within the specific time agreed on by the parties in the contract(s) out of which the controversy has arisen, the matter may not be reopened unless the parties agree on an extension of time. When no specific date is fixed in the contract, the arbitrator may reopen the hearing and shall have thirty days from the closing of the reopened hearing within which to make an award.

38. Waiver of Oral Hearing

Where each party's claim does not exceed $5,000, exclusive of interest and costs, the dispute shall be resolved by submission of documents, unless any party requests an oral hearing, or the arbitrator determines that an oral hearing is necessary. The parties may also provide, by written agreement, for the waiver of oral hearings in any case. If the parities are unable to agree as to the procedure, the AAA shall specify a fair and equitable procedure.

39. Waiver of Rules

Any party who proceeds with the arbitration after knowledge that any provision or requirement of these rules has not been complied with and who fails to state an objection in writing shall be deemed to have waived the right to object.

40. Extensions of Time

The parties may modify any period of time by mutual agreement. The AAA or the arbitrator may for good cause extend any period of time established by these rules, except the time for making the award. The AAA shall notify the parties of any extension.

41. Serving of Notice

Each party shall be deemed to have consented that any papers, notices, or process necessary or proper for the initiation or continuation of an arbitration under these rules; for any court action in connection therewith; or for the entry of judgment on any award made under these rules may be served on a party by mail addressed to the party or its representative at the last known address or by personal service, in or outside the state where the arbitration is to be held, provided that reasonable opportunity to be heard with regard thereto has been granted to the party.

The AAA and the parties may also use facsimile transmission, telex, telegram or other written forms of electronic communication to give the notices required by these rules.

42. The Award

(a) The arbitrator shall endeavor to issue the award promptly and, unless otherwise agreed by the parties, within 30 days from the date of closing of the hearing or, if oral hearings have been waived, from the date of the AAA's transmittal of the final statements and proofs to the arbitrator.

(b) The award shall be in writing, shall be signed by a majority of the arbitrators, and shall be executed in the manner required by law. The award shall contain the names of the parties and representatives, if any, a summary of the issues, including type(s) of any security or product in controversy, the damages and/or other relief requested and awarded, a statement of any other issues resolved, a statement regarding the disposition of any statutory claim, the names of arbitrators, the date when the case was filed, the date of the award, the number and dates of hearings, the location of the hearings, and the signatures of the arbitrators concurring in or dissenting from the award.

(c) The arbitrator may grant any remedy or relief that the arbitrator deems just and equitable and within the scope of the agreement of the parties, including, but not limited to, specific performance of a contract. The arbitrator shall, in the award, assess arbitration fees, expenses, and compensation as provided in Sections 46, 47 and 48 in favor of any party and, in the event that any administrative fees or expenses are due the AAA, in favor of the AAA.

(d) If the parties settle their dispute during the course of the arbitration, the arbitrator may, upon the written agreement of those parties, set forth the terms of the agreed settlement in an award. Such an award is called a consent award.

(e) Parties shall accept as legal delivery of the award the placing of the award or a true copy thereof in the mail addressed to a party or its representative at the last known address, personal service of the award, or the filing of the award in any other manner that is permitted by law.

(f) An award issued under these rules shall be publicly available provided that the names of the parties will not be publicly available.

43. Correction of Award

Within 20 days after the transmittal of an award, any party, upon notice to the other parties, may request that the arbitrator correct any clerical, typographical, technical or computational error in the award. The arbitrator is not empowered to redetermine the merits of any claim already decided.

The other parties shall be given 10 days to respond to the request. The arbitrator shall dispose of the request within 20 days after transmittal by the AAA to the arbitrator of the request and any response thereto.

44. Release of Documents for Judicial Proceedings

The AAA shall, upon the written request of a party, furnish to the party, at its expense, certified copies of any papers in the AAA's possession that may be required in judicial proceedings relating to the arbitration.

45. Applications to Court and Exclusion of Liability

(a) No judicial proceeding by a party relating to the subject matter of the arbitration shall be deemed a waiver of the party's right to arbitrate.

(b) Neither the AAA nor any arbitrator in a proceeding under these rules is a necessary party in judicial proceedings relating to the arbitration.

(c) Parties to these rules shall be deemed to have consented that judgment upon the arbitration award may be entered in any federal or state court having jurisdiction thereof.

(d) Neither the AAA nor any arbitrator shall be liable to any party for any act or omission in connection with any arbitration conducted under these rules.

46. Administrative Fees

As a not-for-profit organization, the AAA shall prescribe filing and other administrative fees to compensate it for the cost of providing administrative services. The fees in effect when the demand for arbitration or submission agreement is received shall be applicable.

The filing fee shall be advanced by the initiating party or parties, subject to final apportionment by the arbitrator in the award.

The AAA may, in the event of extreme hardship on the part of any party, defer or reduce the administrative fees.

47. Expenses

Unless the parties agree otherwise, all expenses of the arbitration, including required travel and other expenses of the arbitrator and AAA representatives, and the cost of any proof produced at the direct request of the arbitrator, shall be borne equally by the parties, subject to final allocation by the arbitrator as provided in Section 42(c).

48. Neutral Arbitrator's Compensation

Unless the parties agree otherwise, members of the National Panel of Securities Arbitrators will receive compensation for the first and second days of service at the rate of $400 per day per arbitrator, advanced equally by the parties.

For service thereafter, an appropriate daily rate and other arrangements will be discussed by the administrator with the parties prior to the appointment of the arbitrator. If the parties fall to agree to the terms of compensation, an appropriate rate will be established by the AAA and communicated in writing to the parties.

49. Deposits

The AAA may require the parties to deposit in advance of any hearings such sums of money as it deems necessary to cover the expense of the arbitration, including the arbitrator's fee, if any, and shall render an accounting to the parties and return any unexpended balance at the conclusion of the case.

50. Interpretation and Application of Rules

The arbitrator shall interpret and apply these rules in so far as they relate to the arbitrator's powers and duties. When there is more than one arbitrator and a difference arises among them concerning the meaning or application of these rules, it shall be decided by a majority vote. If that is not possible, either an arbitrator or a party may refer the question to the AAA for final decision. All other rules shall be interpreted and applied by the AAA.

51. Notice by Telephone

The parties shall accept all notices from the AAA by telephone. Such notices by the AAA shall subsequently be confirmed in writing to the parties. Should there be a failure to confirm in writing any notice hereunder, the proceeding shall nonetheless be valid if notice has, in fact, been given by telephone.

52. Appointment and Qualifications

The AAA shall submit simultaneously to each party an identical list of five proposed arbitrators drawn from the National Panel of Securities

Arbitrators, from which one arbitrator shall be appointed. The arbitrators contained on the list will not be affiliated with the securities industry.

Each party may strike two names from the list on a peremptory basis. The list is returnable to the AAA within 20 days from the date of the AAA's transmittal to the parties.

If for any reason the appointment of an arbitrator cannot be made from the list, the AAA may make the appointment from among other members of the panel without the submission of additional lists.

The parties will be given notice by telephone by the AAA of the appointment of the arbitrator, who shall be subject to disqualification for the reasons specified in Section 20. Within seven days, the parties shall notify the AAA, by telephone, of any objection to the arbitrator appointed. Any objection by a party to the arbitrator shall be confirmed in writing to the AAA with a copy to the other party or parties.

53. Date, Time and Place of Hearing

The arbitrator shall set the date, time and place of the hearing. The AAA will notify the parties by telephone, at least seven days in advance of the hearing date. A formal notice of hearing will also be sent by the AAA to the parties.

54. The Hearing

Generally, the hearing shall be completed within one day, unless the dispute is resolved by submission of documents under Section 38. The arbitrator, for good cause shown, may schedule an additional hearing to be held within seven days.

55. Time of Award

Unless otherwise agreed by the parties, the arbitrator shall endeavor to render the award not later than 14 days from the date of the dosing of the hearing.

Administrative Fees

The AAA's administrative charges are based on filing and service fees. Arbitrator compensation, if any, is not included. Unless the parties agree otherwise, arbitrator compensation and administrative fees are subject to allocation by the arbitrator in the award.

Filing Fees

A non refundable filing fee is payable in full by a filing party when a claim, counterclaim, or additional claim is filed, as provided below.

Amount of Claim	Filing Fee
Up to $25,000	$300
Above $25,000 to $50,000	$500
Above $50,000 to $250,000	$1,000
Above $250,000 to $500,000	$2,000
Above $500,000 to $5,000,000	$3,000
Above $5,000,000	$4,000

When no amount can be stated at the time of filing, the filing fee is $1,000, subject to adjustment when the claim or counterclaim is disclosed.

When a claim or counterclaim is not for a monetary amount, an appropriate filing fee will be determined by the AAA.

Hearing Fees

For each day of hearing held before a single arbitrator, an administrative fee of $100 is payable by each party

For each day of hearing held before a multiarbitrator panel, an administrative fee of $150 is payable by each party.

Postponement Fees

A fee of $50 is payable by a party causing a postponement of any hearing scheduled before a single arbitrator.

A fee of $150 is payable by a party causing a postponement of any hearing scheduled before a multiarbitrator panel.

Processing Fees

No processing fee is payable until 180 days after a case is initiated.

On single-arbitrator cases, a processing fee of $150 per party is payable 180 days after the case is initiated, and every 90 days thereafter, until the case is withdrawn or settled or the hearings are closed by the arbitrator.

On multiarbitrator cases, a processing fee of $200 per party is payable 180 days after the case is initiated, and every 90 days thereafter, until the case is withdrawn or settled or the hearings are closed by the arbitrators.

Suspension for Nonpayment

If arbitrator compensation or administrative charges have not been paid in full, the AAA may so inform the parties in order that one of them may make the required payment. If such payments are not made, the arbitrator may order the suspension or termination of the proceedings. If no arbitrator has yet been appointed, the AAA may suspend the proceedings in such a situation.

Hearing Room Rental

Rooms for hearings are available on a rental basis. Check with our local office for availability and rates.

CODE OF ARBITRATION PROCEDURE

[Code adopted effective November 1, 1968]

PART I.   ADMINISTRATIVE PROVISIONS

¶3701   Matters Eligible for Submission

Sec. 1. This Code of Arbitration Procedure is prescribed and adopted pursuant to Article VII, Section 1(a)(3) of the By-Laws of the National Association of Securities Dealers, Inc., (the Association) for the arbitration of any dispute, claim or controversy arising out of or in connection with the business of any member of the Association, with the exception of disputes involving the insurance business of any member which is also an insurance company:

(1) between or among members;

(2) between or among members and public customers, or others; and

(3) between or among members, registered clearing agencies with which the Association has entered into an agreement to utilize the Association's arbitration facilities and procedures, and participants, pledgees or other persons using the facilities of a registered clearing agency, as these terms are defined under the rules of such a registered clearing agency.

[Sec. 1 amended effective May 7, 1991.]

¶3702   National Arbitration Committee

Sec. 2. The Board of Governors of the Association, following the annual election of members to the Board, shall appoint a National Arbitration Committee of such size and composition, including representation from the public at large, as it shall deem appropriate and in the public interest. The Chairman of the Committee shall be named by the Chairman of the Board. The said Committee shall establish and maintain a pool of arbitrators composed of persons from within and without the securities industry.

The Committee shall have the authority to establish appropriate rules, regulations and procedures to govern the conduct of all arbitration matters before the Association. All rules, regulations and procedures and amendments there to promulgated by the Committee must be by a majority vote of all the members of the said Committee. It shall also have such other power and authority as is necessary to effectuate the purposes of this Code.

The Committee shall meet at least once each year and at such other times as are deemed necessary by the Committee.

¶3703   Director of Arbitration

Sec. 3. The Board of Governors of the Association shall appoint a Director of Arbitration who shall be charged with the performance of all administrative duties and functions in connection with matters submitted for arbitration pursuant to this Code. He shall be directly responsible to the National Arbitration Committee and shall report to it at periodic intervals established by the Committee and at such other times as called upon by the Committee to do so.

¶3704   Composition and Appointment of Panels
Sec. 4. The Director of Arbitration shall compose and appoint panels of arbitrators from the existing pool of arbitrators of the Association to conduct the arbitration of any matter which shall be eligible for submission under this Code. The Director of Arbitration may request that the Executive Committee of the National Arbitration Committee undertake the composition and appointment of a panel or undertake consultation with the Executive Committee regarding the composition and appointment of a panel in any circumstances where he determines such action to be appropriate.

- **Resolution of the Board of Governors**
RESOLVED that all persons serving on panels of arbitrators pursuant to Section 4 of the Association's Code of Arbitration Procedure shall be paid an honorarium for each hearing session in which they participate while in the performance of said duties.
The honorarium shall be $150 for a single session, $225 for a double session, $50 for travel to a cancelled hearing, and $50 per day additional honorarium to the chairperson of the panel. The honorarium for a case not requiring a hearing is $75 per case.
(Resolution adopted effective June 14, 1977; amended May 30, 1980; amended February 8, 1982; amended January 14, 1987.)

¶3705   Non-Waiver of Association Objects and Purposes
Sec. 5. The submission of any matter to arbitration under this Code shall in no way limit or preclude any right, action or determination by the Association which it would otherwise be authorized to adopt, administer or enforce.

¶3706   Legal Proceedings
Sec. 6. No party shall, during the arbitration of any matter, prosecute or commence any suit, action or proceeding against any other party touching upon any of the matters referred to arbitration pursuant to this Code.

¶3707   Amendment, Modification or Cancellation of Code
Sec. 7. This Code may, upon a majority vote of the Board of Governors, be altered, amended, modified or canceled.

- **Selected NASD Notice to Members**
Transitional period for implementation of SEC Rule 15c2-2 to cease as of January 1, 1985.
(December 26, 1984)

PART II.   INDUSTRY AND CLEARING CONTROVERSIES

¶3708   Required Submission
Sec. 8. (a) Any dispute, claim or controversy eligible for under Part I of this code between or among members and/or associated persons,

and/or certain others, arising in connection with the business of such member(s) or in connection with the activities of such associated person(s), shall be arbitrated under this Code, at the instance of:

(1) a member against another member;

(2) a member against a person associated with a member or a person associated with a member against a member; and,

(3) a person associated with a member against a person associated with a member.

(b) Any dispute, claim or controversy involving an act or failure to act by a clearing member, a registered clearing agency, or participants, pledgees or other persons using the facilities of a registered clearing agency, under the rules of any registered clearing agency with which the Association has entered into an agreement to utilize the Association's arbitration facilities and procedures shall be arbitrated in accordance with such agreement and the rules of such registered clearing agency.

¶3709   Composition of Panels

Sec. 9. (a) Except as otherwise provided in Section 10 of the Code, in all arbitration matters between or among members and/or persons associated with members, and where the amount in controversy does not exceed $30,000, the Director of Arbitration shall appoint a single arbitrator to decide the matter in controversy. The arbitrator chosen shall be from the securities industry. Upon the request of a party in its initial filing or the arbitrator, the Director of Arbitration shall appoint a panel of three (3) arbitrators, all of whom shall be from the securities industry.

(b) In all arbitration matters between or among members and/or persons associated with members and where the amount in controversy exceeds $30,000, a panel shall consist of three arbitrators, all of whom shall be from the securities industry.

[Amended effective May 10,1989.]

¶3710   Simplified Industry Arbitration

Sec. 10. (a) Any dispute, claim or controversy arising between or among members or associated persons submitted to arbitration under this Code involving a dollar amount not exceeding $10,000, exclusive of attendant costs shall be resolved by an arbitration panel constituted pursuant to the provisions of subsection (1) hereof solely upon the pleadings and documentary evidence filed by the parties, unless one of the parties to the proceeding files with the Office of the Director of Arbitration within ten (10) business days following the filing of the last pleading a request for a hearing of the matter.

(1) In any proceeding pursuant to this section, an arbitration panel shall consist of no fewer than one (1) but no more than three (3) arbitrators, all of whom shall be from within the securities industry.

(2) Notwithstanding the provisions of this section, any member of an arbitration panel constituted pursuant to this section shall be authorized to request the submission of further documentary evidence in a proceeding and any such panel may by majority vote call and conduct a hearing if such is deemed to be necessary.

(b) All awards rendered in proceedings pursuant to subsection (a) hereof shall be made within thirty (30) business days from the date the arbitrators review all of the written statements, documents and other evidentiary material filed by the parties and declare the matter closed. [Amended effective May 10,1989.]

¶3711   Applicability of Uniform Code

Sec. 11. Except as otherwise provided in this Part, the rules and procedures applicable to arbitrations concerning industry and clearing controversies shall be those set forth hereinafter under Part III.

PART III.   UNIFORM CODE OF ARBITRATION

¶3712   Required Submission

Sec. 12. (a) Any dispute, claim or controversy eligible for submission under Part I of this Code between a customer and a member and/or associated person arising in connection with the business of such member or in connection with the activities of such associated persons shall be arbitrated under this Code, as provided by any duly executed and enforceable written agreement or upon the demand of the customer.

(b) Under this Code, the Director of Arbitration, upon approval of the Executive Committee of the National Arbitration Committee or the National Arbitration Committee, shall have the right to decline the use of its arbitration facilities in any dispute, claim or controversy, where, having due regard for the purposes of the Association and intent of this Code such dispute, claim or controversy is not a proper subject matter arbitration.

(c) Claims which arise out of transactions in a readily identifiable market may, by the consent of the Claimant, be referred to the arbitration forum for that market by the Association.

(d) Class Action Claims.

(1) A claim submitted as a class action shall not be eligible for arbitration under this Code at the Association.

(2) Any claim filed by a member or members of a putative or certified class action is also ineligible for arbitration at the Association if the claim is encompassed by a putative or certified class action filed in federal or state court, or is ordered by a court to an arbitral forum not sponsored by a self-regulatory organization for classwide arbitration. However, such claims shall be eligible for arbitration in accordance with Section 12(a) or pursuant to the parties' contractual agreement, if any, if a claimant demonstrates that it has elected not to participate in the putative or certified class action or, if applicable, has complied with any conditions for withdrawing from the class prescribed by the court.

Disputes concerning whether a particular claim is encompassed by a putative or certified class action shall be referred by the Director of Arbitration to a panel of arbitrators in accordance with Section 13 or Section 19 of the Code, as applicable. Either party may elect instead to petition the court with jurisdiction over the putative or certified class action to resolve such disputes. Any such petition to the court must be filed within ten business days of receipt of notice that the Director of Arbitration is referring the dispute to a panel of arbitrators.

(3) No member or associated person shall seek to enforce any agreement to arbitrate against a customer who has initiated in court a putative class action or is a member of a putative or certified class with respect to any claims encompassed by the class action unless and until: (A) the class certification is denied; (B) the class is decertified; (C) the customer is excluded from the class by the court; or (D) the customer elects not to participate in the putative or certified class action or, if applicable, has complied with any conditions for withdrawing from the class prescribed by the court.

(4) No member or associated person shall be deemed to have waived any of its rights under this Code or under any agreement to arbitrate to which it is party except to the extent stated in this paragraph.
[Amended effective January 8, 1992; October 28, 1992.]

- Selected NASD Notices to Members
    84--51 Approval by the SEC of amendment to the Association's Code of Arbitration Procedures to conform to recent amendments of the Uniform Arbitration Code.

(September 28, 1984)

    92--65 SEC Approval of Amendments Concerning Exclusion of Class-Action Matters from Arbitration Proceedings and Requiring That Predispute Arbitration Agreements Include a Notice that Class-Action Matters May Not be Arbitrated

(December 1992)

¶3713   Simplified Arbitration
Sec. 13. (a) Any dispute, claim or controversy, arising between a public customer(s) and an associated person or a member subject to arbitration under this Code involving a dollar amount not exceeding $10,000.00, exclusive of attendant costs and interest, shall be arbitrated as hereinafter provided.

(b) The Claimant shall file with the Director of Arbitration an executed Submission Agreement and a copy of the Statement of Claim of the controversy in dispute and the required deposit, together with documents in support of the Claim. Sufficient additional copies of the Submission Agreement and the Statement of Claim and supporting documents shall be provided to the Director of Arbitration for each party and the arbitrator. The Statement of Claim shall specify the relevant facts the remedies sought and whether or not a hearing is demanded.

(c) The Claimant shall pay a non-refundable filing fee and shall remit a hearing session deposit as specified in Section 43 of this Code upon filing of the Submission Agreement. The final disposition of the fee or deposit shall be determined by the arbitrator.

(d) The Director of Arbitration shall endeavor to serve promptly by mail or otherwise on the Respondent(s) one (1) copy of the Submission Agreement and one (1) copy of the Statement of Claim. Within twenty (20) calendar days from receipt of the Statement of Claim, Respondent(s) shall serve each party with an executed Submission Agreement and a copy of Respondent's Answer. Respondent's executed Submission

100

Agreement and Answer shall also be filed with the Director of Arbitration with sufficient additional copies for the arbitrator(s) along with any deposit required under the schedule of fees for customer disputes. The Answer shall designate all available defenses to the Claim and may set forth any related Counterclaim and/or related Third-Party Claim the Respondent(s) may have against the Claimant or any other person. If the Respondent(s) has interposed a Third-Party Claim, the Respondent(s) shall serve the Third-Party Respondent with an executed Submission Agreement, a copy of Respondent's Answer containing the Third-Party Claim, and a copy of the original Claim filed by the Claimant. The Third-Party Respondent shall respond in the manner herein provided for response to the Claim. If the Respondent(s) files a related Counterclaim exceeding $10,000, the arbitrator may refer the Claim, Counterclaim and/or Third-Party Claim, if any, to a panel of three (3) or five (5) arbitrators in accordance with Section 19 of this Code or, he may dismiss the Counterclaim and/or Third-Party Claim without prejudice to the Counterclaimant(s) and/or Third-Party Claimant(s) pursuing the Counterclaim and/or Third-Party Claim in a separate proceeding. The costs to the Claimant under either proceeding shall in no event exceed the total amount specified in Section 43.

(e) All parties shall serve on all other parties and the Director of Arbitration, with sufficient additional copies for the arbitrator(s), a copy of the Answer, Counterclaim, Third Party Claim, Amended Claim, or other responsive pleading, if any. The Claimant, if a Counterclaim is asserted against him, shall within ten (10) calendar days either (i) serve on each party and on the Director of Arbitration, with sufficient additional copies for the arbitrator(s), a Reply to any Counterclaim or, (ii) if the amount of the Counterclaim exceeds the Claim, shall have the right to file a statement withdrawing the Claim. If the Claimant withdraws the Claim, the proceedings shall be discontinued without prejudice to the rights of the parties.

(f) The dispute, claim or controversy shall be submitted to a single public arbitrator knowledgeable in the securities industry selected by the Director of Arbitration. Unless the public customer demands or consents to a hearing, or the arbitrator calls a hearing, the arbitrator shall decide the dispute, claim or controversy solely upon the pleadings and evidence filed by the parties. If a hearing is necessary, such hearing shall be held as soon as practicable at a locale selected by the Director of Arbitration.

(g) The Director of Arbitration may grant extensions of time to file any pleading upon a showing of good cause.

(h) (i) The arbitrator shall be authorized to require the submission of further documentary evidence as he, in his sole discretion, deems advisable:

(ii) If a hearing is demanded or consented to in accordance with Section 13(f), the General Provisions Governing Pre-Hearing Proceedings under Section 32 shall apply.

(iii) If no hearing is demanded or consented to, all requests for document production shall be submitted in writing to the Director of Arbitration within ten (10) business days of notification of the identity of the arbitrator selected to decide the case. The requesting party shall serve simultaneously its requests for document production on all parties. Any response or objections to the requested document production shall be served on all parties and filed with the Director of Arbitration within five (5) business days of receipt of the requests for production. The selected arbitrator shall resolve all requests under this section on the papers submitted.

(i) Upon the request of the arbitrator, the Director of Arbitration shall appoint two (2) additional arbitrators to the panel which shall decide the matter in controversy.

(j) In any case where there is more than one (1) arbitrator, the majority shall be public arbitrators.

(k) In his discretion, the arbitrator may, at the request of any party, permit such party to submit additional documentation relating to the pleadings.

(l) Except as otherwise provided herein, the general arbitration rules of the association shall be applicable to proceedings instituted under this Section.

[Amended effective October 1, 1984; April 1, 1988; May 10, 1989; June 1, 1990; April 26, 1991; January 8, 1992; September 8, 1992.]

- **Interpretation of the Board of Governors**

Related Counterclaim
As used in this Section 13, the term "related Counterclaim" shall mean any Counterclaim related to a customer's accounts with a member.

¶3714   Hearing Requirements-Waiver of Hearing
Sec. 14. (a) Any dispute, claim or controversy except as provided in Section 10 Simplified Industry Arbitration) or Section 13 (Simplified Arbitration), shall require a hearing unless all parties waive such hearing in writing and request that the matter be resolved solely upon the pleadings and documentary evidence.

(b) Notwithstanding a written waiver of a hearing by the parties, a majority of the arbitrators may call for and conduct a hearing. In addition, any arbitrator may request he submission of further evidence.

¶3715   Time Limitation Upon Submission
Sec. 15. No dispute, claim, or controversy shall be eligible for submission to arbitration under this Code where six (6) years have elapsed from the occurrence or event giving rise to the act or dispute, claim or controversy. This section shall not extend applicable statutes of limitations, nor shall it apply to any case which is directed to arbitration by a court of competent jurisdiction.

[Amended effective October 1, 1984.]

¶3716   Dismissal of Proceedings
Sec. 16. At any time during the course of an arbitration, the arbitrators may, either upon their own initiative or at the request of a party, dismiss the proceeding and refer the parties to the remedies

provided by applicable law. The arbitrators shall at the joint request of all the parties dismiss the proceedings.

¶3717   Settlements

Sec. 17. All settlements upon any matter shall be at the election of the parties.

¶3718   Tolling of Time Limitation(s) for the Institution of Legal Proceedings and Extension of Time Limitation(s) for Submission to Arbitration

Sec. 18. (a) Where permitted by applicable law, the time limitations which would otherwise run or accrue for the institution of legal proceedings shall be tolled where a duly executed Submission Agreement is filed by the Claimant(s). The tolling shall continue for such period as the Association shall retain jurisdiction upon the matter submitted.

(b) The six (6) year time limitation upon submission to arbitration shall not apply when the parties have submitted the dispute, claim or controversy to a court of competent jurisdiction. The six (6) year time limitation shall not run for such period as the court shall retain jurisdiction upon the matter submitted.

[Amended effective October 1, 1984.]

¶3719   Designation of Number of Arbitrators

Sec. 19. (a) Except as otherwise provided in Section 13 in this Code, in all arbitration matters involving public customers and where the amount in controversy does not exceed $30,000, the Director of Arbitration shall appoint a single public arbitrator knowledgeable in but who is not from the securities industry to decide the dispute, claim or controversy. Upon the request of a party in its initial filing or the arbitrator, the Director of Arbitration shall appoint a panel of three (3) arbitrators which shall decide the matter in controversy. At least a majority of the arbitrators appointed shall not be from the securities industry, unless the public customer requests a panel consisting of at least a majority from the securities industry.

(b) In arbitration matters involving public customers and where the amount in controversy exceeds $30,000, or where the matter in controversy does not involve or disclose a money claim, the Director of Arbitration shall appoint an arbitration panel which consists of no fewer than three (3) nor more than five (5) arbitrators, at least a majority of whom shall not be from the securities industry, unless the public customer requests a panel consisting of at least a majority from the securities industry.

(c) An arbitrator will be deemed as being from the securities industry if he or she:

(1) is a person associated with a member or other broker/dealer, municipal securities dealer, government securities broker, or government securities dealer, or

(2) has been associated with any of the above within the past three (3) years, or

(3) is retired from any of the above, or

(4) is an attorney, accountant, or other professional who has devoted twenty (20) percent or more of his or her professional work effort to securities industry clients within the last two years, or

(5) is an individual who is registered under the Commodity Exchange Act or is a member of a registered futures association or any commodities exchange or is associated with any such person(s).

(d) An arbitrator who is not from the securities industry shall be deemed a public arbitrator. A person will not be classified as a public arbitrator if he or she has a spouse or other member of the household who is a person who is associated with a member or other broker/dealer, municipal securities dealer, government securities broker, or government securities dealer.

[Amended effective July 1, 1986; April 1, 1988; May 10, 1989; October 7, 1992.]

¶3720   Composition of Panels

Sec. 20. The individuals who shall serve on a particular arbitration panel shall be determined by the Director of Arbitration. The Director of Arbitration may name the chairman of the panel.

¶3721   Notice of Selection of Arbitrators

Sec. 21. The Director of Arbitration shall inform the parties of the arbitrators names and employment histories for the past ten (10) years, as well as information disclosed pursuant to Section 23, at least eight (8) business days prior to the date fixed for the first hearing session. A party may make further inquiry of the Director of Arbitration concerning an arbitrator's background. In the event that prior to the first hearing session, any arbitrator should become disqualified, resign, die, refuse or otherwise be unable to perform as an arbitrator, the Director of Arbitration shall appoint a replacement arbitrator to fill the vacancy on the panel. The Director of Arbitration shall inform the parties as soon as possible of the name and employment history of the replacement arbitrator for the past ten years, as well as information disclosed pursuant to Section 23. A party may make further inquiry of the Director of Arbitration concerning the replacement arbitrator's background and within the time remaining prior to the first hearing session or the five (5) day period provided under Section 22, whichever is shorter, may exercise its right to challenge the replacement arbitrator as provided in Section 22.

[Amended effective September 19, 1988; May 10, 1989.]

¶3722   Peremptory Challenge

Sec. 22. In any arbitration proceeding, each party shall have the right to one peremptory challenge. In arbitrations where there are multiple Claimants, Respondents and/or Third-Party Respondents, the Claimants shall have one peremptory challenge, the Respondents shall have one peremptory challenge and the Third-Party Respondents shall have one peremptory challenge, unless the Director of Arbitration determines that the interests of justice would best be served by awarding additional peremptory challenges. Unless extended by the Director of Arbitration, a party wishing to exercise a peremptory challenge must

do so by notifying the Director of Arbitration in writing within five (5) business days of notification of the identity of the person(s) named under Section 21 or Section 32(d) or (e), whichever comes first. There shall be unlimited challenges for cause.
[Amended effective October 1,1984; January 8, 1992.]

¶3723   Disclosures Required of Arbitrators
Sec. 23. (a) Each arbitrator shall be required to disclose to the Director of Arbitration any circumstances which might preclude such arbitrator from rendering an objective and impartial determination. Each arbitrator shall disclose:
(1) Any direct or indirect financial or personal interest in the outcome of the arbitration;
(2) Any existing or past financial, business, professional, family, or social relationships that are likely to affect impartiality or might reasonably create an appearance of partiality or bias. Persons requested to serve as arbitrators should disclose any such relationships that they personally have with any party or its counsel, or with any individual whom they have been told will be a witness. They should also disclose any such relationship involving members of their families or their current employers, partners, or business associates.
(b) Persons who are requested to accept appointment as arbitrators should make a reasonable effort to inform themselves of any interests or relationships described in Paragraph (a) above.
(c) The obligation to disclose interests, relationships, or circumstances that might preclude an arbitrator from rendering an objective and impartial determination described in subsection (a) hereof is a continuing duty that requires a person who accepts appointment as an arbitrator to disclose, at any stage of the arbitration, any such interests, relationships, or circumstances that arise, or are recalled or discovered.
(d) Prior to the commencement of the first hearing session, the Director of Arbitration may remove an arbitrator based on information disclosed pursuant to this section. The Director of Arbitration shall also inform the parties of any information disclosed pursuant to this Section if the arbitrator who disclosed the information is not removed.
[Amended effective May 10,1989.]

¶3724   Disqualification or Other Disability of Arbitrators
Sec. 24. In the event that any arbitrator, after the commencement of the first hearing session but prior to the rendition of the award, should become disqualified, resign, die, refuse or otherwise be unable to perform as an arbitrator, the remaining arbitrator(s) shall continue with the hearing and determination of the controversy, unless such continuation is objected to by any party within five (5) days of notification of the vacancy on the panel. Upon objection, the Director of Arbitration shall appoint a replacement arbitrator to fill the vacancy and the hearing shall continue. The Director of Arbitration shall inform the parties as soon as possible of the name and employment history of the replacement arbitrator for the past ten years, as well as information disclosed pursuant to Section 23. A party may make further inquiry of the Director of Arbitration concerning the replacement arbitrator's background and

within the time remaining prior to the next scheduled hearing session or the five (5) day period provided under Section 22, whichever is shorter, may exercise its right to challenge the replacement arbitrator as provided in Section 22.

[Amended effective September 19, 1988.]

¶3725 Initiation of Proceedings

Sec. 25. Except as otherwise provided herein, an arbitration proceeding under this Code shall be instituted as follows:

Statement of Claim

(a) The Claimant shall file with the Director of Arbitration an executed Submission Agreement, a Statement of Claim of the controversy in dispute, together with the documents in support of the Claim and the required deposit. Sufficient additional copies of the Submission Agreement and the Statement of Claim and supporting documents shall be provided to the Director of Arbitration for each party and each arbitrator. The Statement of Claim shall specify the relevant facts and the remedies sought. The Director of Arbitration shall endeavor to serve promptly by mail or otherwise on the Respondent(s) one (1) copy of the Submission Agreement and one (1) copy of the Statement of Claim.

Answer-Defenses, Counterclaims and/or Cross-Claims

(b)(1) Within twenty (20) business days from receipt of the Statement of Claim, Respondent(s) shall serve each party with an executed Submission Agreement and a copy of Respondent's Answer. Respondent's executed Submission Agreement and Answer shall also be filed with the Director of Arbitration with sufficient additional copies for the arbitrator(s) along with any deposit required under the schedule of fees. The Answer shall specify all available defenses and relevant facts thereto that will be relied upon at hearing and may set forth any related Counterclaim the Respondent(s) may have against the Claimant, any Cross-Claim the Respondent(s) may have against any other named Respondent(s), and any Third-Party Claim against any other party or person based upon any existing dispute, claim or controversy subject to arbitration under this Code

(2)(i) A Respondent, Responding Claimant, Cross-Claimant, Cross-Respondent, or Third-Party Respondent who pleads only a general denial as an answer may, upon objection by a party, in the discretion of the arbitrators, be barred from presenting any facts or defenses at the time of the hearing.

(ii) A Respondent, Responding Claimant, Cross-Claimant, Cross-Respondent, or Third-Party Respondent who fails to specify all available defenses and relevant facts in such party's answer may, upon objection by a party, in the discretion of the arbitrators, be barred from presenting such facts or defenses not included in such party's answer at the hearing.

(iii) A Respondent, Responding Claimant, Cross-Claimant, Cross-Respondent, or Third-Party Respondent who fails to file an answer within twenty (20) business days from receipt of service of a claim, unless the time to answer has been extended pursuant to paragraph (5), below, may, in the discretion of the arbitrators, be barred from presenting any matter, arguments or defenses at the hearing.

(3) Respondent(s) shall serve each party with a copy of any Third-Party Claim. The Third Party Claim shall also be filed with the Director of Arbitration with sufficient additional copies for the arbitrator(s) along with any deposit required under the schedule of fees. Third-Party Respondent(s) shall answer in the manner provided for response to the Claim, as provided in paragraphs (1) and (2) above.

(4) The Claimant shall serve each party with a Reply to a Counter-claim within ten (10) days of receipt of an Answer containing a Counter-claim. The Reply shall also be filed with the Director of Arbitration with sufficient additional copies for the arbitrator(s).

(5) The time period to file any pleading, whether such be denomi-nated as a Claim, Answer, Counterclaim, Cross-claim, Reply, or Third-Party pleading, may be extended for such further period as may be granted by the Director of Arbitration.

Service and Filing With the Director of Arbitration

(c)(1) Service may be effected by mail or other means of delivery. Service and filing are accomplished on the date of mailing either by first-class postage pre-paid or by means of overnight mail service or, in the case of other means of service, on the date of delivery. Filing with the Director of Arbitration shall be made on the same date as service on a party.

(2) If a member firm and a person associated with the member firm are named parties to an arbitration proceeding at the time of the filing of the Statement of Claim, service on the person associated with the member firm may be made on the associated person or the member firm, which shall perfect service upon the associated person. If the member firm does not undertake to represent the associated person, the member firm shall serve the associated person with the Statement of Claim, shall advise all parties and the Director of Arbitration of that fact, and shall provide such associated person's current address.

Joinder and Consolidation-Multiple Parties

(d)(1) Permissive Joinder. All persons may join in one action as claimants if they assert any right to relief jointly, severally, or arising out of the same transaction, occurrence or series of transactions or occur-rences and if any questions of law or fact common to all these claimants will arise in the action. All persons may be joined in one action as respondents if there is asserted against them jointly or severally, any right to relief arising out of the same transaction, occurrence or series of transactions or occurrences and if any questions of law or fact common to all respondents will arise in the action. A claimant or respondent need not assert rights to or defend against all the relief demanded. Judgment may be given for one or more of the claimants according to their respective rights to relief, and against one or more respondents according to the irrespective liabilities.

(2) In arbitrations where there are multiple Claimants, Respondents and/or Third Party Respondents, the Director of Arbitration shall be

authorized to determine preliminarily whether such parties should proceed in the same or separate arbitrations. Such determination will be considered subsequent to the filing of all responsive pleadings.

(3) The Director of Arbitration shall be authorized to determine preliminarily whether claims filed separately are related and shall be authorized to consolidate such claims for hearing and award purposes.

(4) Further determinations with respect to joinder, consolidation, and multiple parties under this subsection shall be made by the arbitration panel and shall be deemed final.

[Amended effective October 1, 1984; July 1, 1986; May 10, 1989; May 7, 1991.]

¶3726   Designation of Time and Place of Hearings
Sec. 26. The time and place of the initial hearing shall be determined by the Director of Arbitration and each hearing thereafter by the arbitrators. Notice of the time and place for the initial hearing shall be given at least eight (8) business days prior to the date fixed for the hearing by personal service, registered or certified mail to each of the parties unless the parties shall, by their mutual consent, waive the notice provisions under this Section. Notice for each hearing thereafter shall be given as the arbitrators may determine. Attendance at a hearing waives notice thereof.

[Amended effective May 7, 1991.]

¶3727   Representation by Counsel
Sec. 27. All parties shall have the right to representation by counsel at any stage of the proceedings.

¶3728   Attendance at Hearings
Sec. 28. The attendance or presence of all persons at hearings including witnesses shall be determined by the arbitrators. However, all parties to the arbitration and their counsel shall be entitled to attend all hearings.

• Policy of the Board of Governors
In response to recent questions concerning the order of closing argument in arbitration proceedings conducted under the auspices of the National Association of Securities Dealers, Inc., it is the practice in these proceedings to allow claimants to proceed first in closing argument, with rebuttal argument being permitted. Claimants may reserve their entire closing for rebuttal. The hearing procedures may, however, be varied in the discretion of the arbitrators, provided all parties are allowed a full and fair opportunity to present their respective cases.

¶3729   Failure to Appear
Sec. 29. If any of the parties, after due notice, fails to appear at a hearing or at any continuation of a hearing session, the arbitrators may, in their discretion, proceed with the arbitration of the controversy. In such cases, all awards shall be rendered as if each party had entered an appearance in the matter submitted.

[Amended effective January 8, 1992.]

¶3730   Adjournments

Sec. 30. (a) The arbitrator(s) may, in their discretion, adjourn any hearing(s) whether upon their own initiative or upon the request of any party to the arbitration.

(b) Unless waived by the Director of Arbitration upon a showing of financial need, party requesting an adjournment after arbitrators have been appointed shall deposit with the request for an adjournment, a fee equal to the initial deposit of hearing session fees for the first adjournment and twice the initial deposit of hearing session fees, not to exceed $1,000, for a second or subsequent adjournment requested by that party. If the adjournment is not granted, the deposit shall he refunded. If the adjournment is not granted, the arbitrator(s) may direct the return of the adjournment fee.

(c) Upon receiving a third request consented to by all parties for an adjournment, the arbitrator(s) may dismiss the arbitration without prejudice to the Claimant filing a arbitration.

[Amended effective July 1, 1986; June 1, 1990; December 30, 1991.]

¶3731   Acknowledgement of Pleadings

Sec. 31. The arbitrators shall acknowledge to all parties present that they have read the pleadings filed by the parties.

¶3732   General Provisions Governing Pre-Hearing Proceedings

Sec. 32. (a) Requests for Documents and Information. The parties shall cooperate to the fullest extent practicable in the voluntary exchange of documents and information to expedite the arbitration. Any request for documents or other information should be specific, relate to the matter in controversy, and afford the party to whom the request is made a reasonable period of time to respond without interfering with time set for the hearing.

(b) Document Production and Information Exchange.

(1) Any party may serve a written request for information or documents ("information request") upon another party twenty (20) business days or more after service of the Statement of Claim by the Director of Arbitration or upon filing of the Answer, whichever is earlier. The requesting party shall serve the information request on all parties and file a copy with the Director of Arbitration. The parties shall endeavor to resolve disputes regarding an information request prior to serving any objection to the request. Such efforts shall be set forth in the objection.

(2) Unless a greater time is allowed by the requesting party, information requests shall be satisfied or objected to within thirty (30) calendar days from the date of service. Any objection to an information request shall be served by the objecting party on all parties and filed with the Director of Arbitration.

(3) Any response to objections to an information request shall be served on all parties and filed with the Director of Arbitration within ten (10) calendar days of receipt of the objection.

(4) Upon the written request of a party whose information request is unsatisified, the matter will be referred by the Director of Arbitration to either a pre-hearing conference under subsection

(d) of this section or to a selected arbitrator under subsection (e) of this section.

(c) Pre-Hearing Exchange. At least ten (10) calendar days prior to the first scheduled hearing date, all parties shall serve on each other copies of documents in their possession they intend to present at the hearing and shall identify witnesses they intend to present at the hearing. The arbitrators may exclude from the arbitration any documents not exchanged or witnesses not identified. This paragraph does not require service of copies of documents or identification of witnesses which parties may use for cross-examination or rebuttal.

(d) Pre-Hearing Conference

(1) Upon the written request of a party, an arbitrator, or at the discretion of the Director of Arbitration, a pre-hearing conference shall be scheduled. The Director of Arbitration shall set the time and place of a pre-hearing conference and appoint a person to preside. The pre-hearing conference may be held by telephone conference call. The presiding person shall seek to achieve agreement among the parties on any issue which relates to the pre-hearing process or to the hearing, including but not limited to exchange of information, exchange or production of documents, identification of witnesses, identification and exchange of hearing documents, stipulation of facts, identification and briefing of contested issues, and any other matters which will expedite the arbitration proceedings.

(2) Any issues raised at the pre-hearing conference that are not resolved maybe referred to a single member of the arbitration panel for decision.

(e) Decisions by Selected Arbitrator. The Director of Arbitration may appoint a single member of the arbitration panel to decide all unresolved issues under this section. In matters involving public customers, such single arbitrator shall be a public arbitrator, except that the arbitrator may be either public or industry when the public customer has requested a panel consisting of a majority from the securities industry. Such arbitrator shall be authorized to act on behalf of the panel to issue subpoenas, direct appearances of witnesses and production of documents, set deadlines for compliance, and issue any other ruling which will expedite the arbitration proceedings. Decisions under this section shall be made upon the papers submitted by the parties, unless the arbitrator calls a hearing. The arbitrator may elect to refer any issue under this section to the full panel.

[Amended effective May 10, 1989.]

¶3733   Subpoenas and Power to Direct Appearances

Sec. 33. (a) Subpoenas. The arbitrators and any counsel of record to the proceeding shall have the power of the subpoena process as provided by law. All parties shall be given a copy of a subpoena upon its issuance. Parties shall produce witnesses and present proofs to the fullest extent possible without resort to the subpoena process.

(b) Power to Direct Appearances and Production of Documents. The arbitrator(s)shall be empowered without resort to the subpoena process

to direct the appearance of any person employed or associated with any member of the Association and/or the production of any records in the possession or control of such persons or members. Unless the arbitrator(s) direct otherwise, the party requesting the appearance of a person or the production of documents under this Section shall bear all reasonable costs of such appearance and/or production.
[Amended effective May 10, 1989.]

¶3734   Evidence
Sec. 34. The arbitrators shall determine the materiality and relevance of any evidence proffered and shall not be bound by rules governing the admissibility of evidence.

¶3735   Interpretation of Provisions of Code and Enforcement of Arbitrator Rulings
Sec. 35. The arbitrators shall be empowered to interpret and determine the applicability of all provisions under this Code and to take appropriate action to obtain compliance with any ruling by the arbitrator(s). Such interpretations and actions to obtain compliance shall be final and binding upon the parties.
[Amended effective November 16, 1992.]

¶3736   Determination of Arbitrators
Sec. 36. All rulings and determinations of the panel shall be by a majority of the arbitrators.

¶3737   Record of Proceedings
Sec. 37. A verbatim record by stenographic reporter or tape recording of all arbitration hearings shall be kept. If a party or parties to a dispute elect to have the record transcribed, the cost of such transcription shall be borne by the party or parties making the request unless the arbitrators direct otherwise. The arbitrators may also direct that the record be transcribed. If the record is transcribed at the request of any party, a copy shall be provided to the arbitrators.
[Amended effective May 10, 1989.]

¶3738   Oaths of the Arbitrators and Witnesses
Sec. 38. Prior to the commencement of the first session, an oath or affirmation shall be administered to the arbitrators. All testimony shall be under oath or affirmation.

¶3739   Amendments
Sec. 39. (a) After the filing of any pleadings, if a party desires to file a new or different pleading, such change must be made in writing and filed with the Director of Arbitration with sufficient additional copies for each arbitrator. The party filing a new or different pleading shall serve on all other parties, a copy of the new or different pleading in accordance with the provisions set forth in Section 25(b). The other parties may, within ten (10) business days from the receipt of service, file a response with all other parties and the Director of Arbitration in accordance with Section 25(b).

(b) After a panel has been appointed, 110 new or different pleading may be filed except for a responsive pleading as provided for in (a) above or with the panel's consent.

[Amended effective October 1, 1984; April 26, 1991.]

¶3740   Reopening of Hearings

Sec. 40. Where permitted by applicable law, the hearings may be reopened by the arbitrators on their own motion or in the discretion of the arbitrators upon application of a party at any time before the award is rendered.

¶3741   Awards

Sec. 41. (a) All awards shall be in writing and signed by a majority of the arbitrators or in such manner as is required by applicable law. Such awards may be entered as a judgment in any court of competent jurisdiction.

(b) Unless the applicable law directs otherwise, all awards rendered pursuant to this Code shall be deemed final and not subject to review or appeal.

(c) The Director of Arbitration shall endeavor to serve a copy of the award: (i) by registered or certified mail upon all parties, or their counsel, at the address of record; or, (ii) by personally serving the award upon the parties; or, (iii) by filing or delivering the award in such manner as may be authorized by law.

(d) The arbitrator(s) shall endeavor to render an award within thirty (30) business days from the date the record is closed.

(e) The award shall contain the names of the party the name of counsel, if any, a summary of the issues, including the type(s) of any security or product in controversy, the damages and other relief requested, the damages and other relief a statement of any other issues resolved, the names of the arbitrators, the dates the claim was filed and the award rendered, the number and dates of hearing sessions, the location of the hearings, and the signatures of the arbitrators concurring in the award.

(f) All awards involving public customers and their contents, excluding the names of the arbitrators, shall be made publicly available. A party to an arbitration involving a public customer may request that the Director of Arbitration provide copies of all awards rendered by the arbitrator(s) chosen to decide its case. A party wishing to obtain such information must notify the Director of Arbitration within three (3) business days of receipt of notification of the identity of the person(s) named to the panel.

(g) Fees and assessments imposed by the arbitrators under Sections 43 and 44 shall be paid immediately upon the receipt of the award by the parties. Payment of such fees shall not be deemed ratification of the award by the parties.

(h) All monetary awards shall be paid within thirty (30) days of receipt unless a motion to vacate has been filed with a court of competent jurisdiction. An award shall bear interest from the date of award: (i) if not paid within thirty (30) days of receipt, (ii) if the award is the subject of a motion to vacate which is denied, or (iii) as specified by the arbitrator(s) in the award. Interest shall be assessed at the legal rate, if any, then prevailing in the state where the award was rendered, or at a rate set by the arbitrator(s).

[Amended effective May 10, 1989; April 26, 1991; May 7, 1991; January 8, 1992.]

¶3742　Incorporation By Reference

Sec. 42. This Code shall be deemed a part of and incorporated by reference in every agreement to arbitrate under the rules of the National Association of Securities Dealers, Inc. including a duly executed Submission Agreement.

[Amended effective May 7,1991.]

¶3743　Schedule of Fees for Customer Disputes

Sec. 43. (a) At the time of filing a Claim, Counterclaim, Third Party Claim or Cross-Claim, a party shall pay a non-refundable filing fee and shall remit a hearing session deposit to the Association in the amounts indicated in the schedules below unless such fee or deposit is specifically waived by the Director of Arbitration.

Where multiple hearing sessions are required, the arbitrators may require any of the parties to make additional hearing deposits for each additional hearing session. In no event shall the amount deposited by all parties per hearing session exceed the amount of the largest initial hearing deposit made by any party under the schedules below.

(b) A hearing session is any meeting between the parties and the arbitrator(s), including a pre-hearing conference with an arbitrator, which lasts four (4) hours or less. The forum fee for a pre-hearing conference with an arbitrator shall be the amount set forth in the schedules below as a hearing session deposit for a hearing with a single arbitrator.

(c) The arbitrators, in their awards shall determine the amount chargeable to the parties as forum fees and shall determine who shall pay such forum fees. Forum fees agreable to the parties shall he assessed on a per hearing session basis, and the aggregate for each hearing session may equal but shall not exceed the amount of the largest initial hearing deposit deposited by any party, except in a case where claims have been joined subsequent to filing in which case hearing session fees shall he computed as provided in paragraph (d). The arbitrator(s) may determine in the award at a party shall reimburse to another party any non-refundable filing fee it has paid. If a customer is assessed forum fees in connection with an industry claim, forum fees assessed against the customer shall be based on the hearing deposit required under the industry claims schedule for the amount awarded to industry parties to be paid by the customer and not based on the size of the industry claim. No fees shall be assessed against a customer in connection with an industry claim that is dismissed; however, in cases where there is also a customer claim, the customer may be assessed forum fees based on the customer claim under the procedure set out above. Amounts deposited by party shall be applied against forum fees, if any. In addition to forum fees, the arbitrator(s) may determine in the award the amount of costs incurred pursuant to actions 30, 32, 33, and 37 and, unless applicable

113

law directs otherwise, other costs and expenses of the parties and arbitrator(s) which are within the scope of the agreement of the parties. The arbitrator(s) shall determine by whom such costs shall be borne. If the hearing session fees are not assessed against a party who had made a hearing deposit, the hearing deposit will be refunded unless the arbitrators determine otherwise.

(d) For claims filed separately which are subsequently joined or consolidated under action 25(d) of this Code, the hearing deposit and forum fees assessable per hearing session after joinder or consolidation shall be based on the cumulative amount in dispute. The arbitrator(s) shall determine by whom such fees shall be borne.

(e) If the dispute, claim, or controversy does not involve, disclose, or specify a money claim, the non-refundable filing fee shall be $250 and the hearing session deposit be remitted by a party shall be $600 or such greater or lesser amount as the Director Arbitration or the panel of arbitrators may require, but shall not exceed $1,000.

(f) The Association shall retain the total initial amount deposited as hearing session deposits by all the parties in any matter submitted and settled or withdrawn within eight business days of the first scheduled hearing session other than a prehearing conference.

(g) Any matter submitted and thereafter settled or withdrawn subsequent to the commencement of the first hearing session, including a pre-hearing conference with an arbitrator, shall be subject to an assessment of forum fees and costs incurred pursuant Sections 30, 32, 33, and 37 based on hearing sessions held and scheduled within eight business days after the Association receives notice that the matter has been settled or withdrawn. The arbitrator(s) shall determine by whom such forum fees and costs shall borne.

Schedule of Fees

For purposes of the schedule of fees, the term "claim" includes Claims, Counter Claims, Third Party Claims, and Cross-Claims. Any such claim made by a customer is a customer claim. Any such claim made by a member or associated person of a member is an industry claim.

Customer Claimant

Amount in Dispute (Exclusive of Interest and Expenses)	Claim Filing Fee	Hearing Session Deposit		
		Simplified[1]	One Arbitrator[2]	Three + Arbitrator[3]
$0.01--$1,000	$15	$15	$15	NA
$1000.01--$2,500	$25	$25	$25	NA
$2,500.01--$5,000	$50	$75	$100	NA
$5,000.01--$10,000	$75	$75	$200	NA
$10,000.01--$30,000	$100	NA	$300	$400
$30,000.01--$50,000	$120	NA	$300[4]	$400
$50,000.01--$100,000	$150	NA	$300[4]	$500
$100,000.01--$500,000	$200	NA	$300[4]	$750
$500,000.01--$5,000,000	$250	NA	$300[4]	$1000
Over $5,000,000	$300	NA	$300[4]	$1500

[1]Simplified Arbitration (Without Hearing)

Industry Claimant

Amount in Dispute (Exclusive of Interest and Expenses)	Claim Filing Fee	Hearing Session Deposit		
		Simplified[1]	One Arbitrator[2]	Three + Arbitrators[3]
$0.01--$1,000	$500	$75	$300	NA
$1000.01--$2,500	$500	$75	$300	NA
$2,500.01--$5,000	$500	$75	$300	NA
$5,000.01--$10,000	$500	$75	$300	NA
$10,000.01--$30,000	$500	NA	$300	$400
$30,000.01--$50,000	$500	NA	$300[4]	$400
$50,000.01--$100,000	$500	NA	$300[4]	$500
$100,000.01--$500,000	$500	NA	$300[4]	$750
$500,000.01--$5,000,000	$500	NA	$300[4]	$1000
Over $5,000,000	$500	NA	$300[4]	$1500

[1]Simplified Arbitration (Without Hearing)
[2]One Arbitrator (Per Hearing Session)
[3]Three or more Arbitrators (Per Hearing Session)
[4]Prehearing Conferences Only

[Amended effective October 1, 1984; July 1, 1987; April 1, 1988; May 10, 1989, June 1, 1990.]

- ## Resolution of the Board of Governors

¶3744   Failure to Act Under Provisions of Code of Arbitration Procedure

It may be deemed conduct inconsistent with just and equitable principles of trade and a violation of Article III Section 1 of the Rules of Fair Practice for a member or a person associated with a member to fail to submit a dispute for arbitration under the NASD Code of Arbitration Procedure as required by that Code, to fail to appear or to produce any document in his possession or control as directed pursuant to provisions of the NASD Code of Arbitration Procedure, or to fail to honor an award of arbitrators properly rendered pursuant to the Uniform Code of Arbitration under the auspices of the National Association of Securities Dealers, Inc., the New York, American, Boston, Cincinnati, Midwest, Pacific, or Philadelphia Stock Exchanges, the Chicago Board Options Exchange, the Municipal Securities Rule Making Board, or pursuant to the rules applicable to the arbitration of securities disputes before the American Arbitration Association, where a timely motion has not been made to vacate or modify such award pursuant to applicable law.

All awards shall be honored by a cash payment to the prevailing, party of the exact dollar amount stated in the award. Awards may not be honored by crediting the prevailing party's account with the dollar amount of the award, unless authorized by the express terms of the award or consented to in writing by the parties. Awards shall be honored upon receipt thereof, or within such other time period as may be prescribed by the award.

Action by members requiring associated persons to waive the arbitration of disputes contrary to the provisions of the Code of Arbitration Procedure shall constitute conduct that is inconsistent with just and equitable principles of trade and a violation of Article III, Section 1 of the Rules of Fair Practice.

(Resolution adopted effective May 1,1973 and amended July 1,1987; May 7,1991.)

- Selected NASD Notices to Members

87--55 Amendments to NASD Code of Arbitration Procedure effective July 1,1987.

(August 14,1987)

88--14 Additional Arbitration Filing Fee and Advertising Service Charge.

(February 10, 1988)

¶3746   Schedule of Fees for Industry and Clearing Controversies

Sec. 44. (a) At the time of filing a Claim, Counterclaim, Third-Party Claim or a Cross-Claim in an industry or clearing controversy which is required to be submitted to arbitration before the Association as set forth in Section 8, above, a party shall pay a non-refundable filing fee and shall remit a hearing session deposit to the Association in the amounts indicated in the schedule below unless such fee or deposit is specifically waived by the Director of Arbitration.

Where multiple hearing sessions are required, the arbitrator(s) may require any of the parties to make additional hearing deposits for each additional hearing session. In no event shall the amount deposited by all parties per hearing session exceed the amount of the largest initial hearing deposit made by any party under the schedule below.

(b) A hearing session is any meeting between the parties and the arbitrator(s), including a pre-hearing conference with an arbitrator, which lasts four (4) hours or less. The forum fee for a pre-hearing conference with an arbitrator shall be the amount set forth in the schedule below as a hearing session deposit for a hearing with a single arbitrator.

(c) The arbitrators, in their award, shall determine the amount chargeable to the parties as forum fees and shall determine who shall pay such forum fees. Forum fees chargeable to the parties shall be assessed on a per hearing session basis and the aggregate for each hearing session may equal but shall not exceed the amount of the largest initial hearing deposit deposited by any party, except in a case where claims have been joined subsequent to filing in which case hearing session fees shall be computed as provided in paragraph (d). The arbitrator(s) may determine in the award that a party shall reimburse to another party any non-refundable filing fee it has paid. Amounts deposited by a party shall be applied against forum fees, if any. In addition to forum fees, the arbitrator(s) may determine in the award the amount of costs incurred pursuant to Sections 30, 32, 33, and 37 and, unless applicable law directs otherwise other costs and expenses of the parties and arbitrator(s) which are within the scope of the agreement of the parties. The arbitrator(s) shall determine by whom such costs shall be borne. If the hearing session fees are not assessed against a party who had made a hearing deposit, the hearing deposit will be refunded unless the arbitrators determine otherwise.

(d) For claims filed separately which are subsequently joined or consolidated under Section 25(d) of this Code, the hearing deposit and forum fees assessable per hearing session after joinder or consolidation shall be based on the cumulative amount in dispute. The arbitrator(s) shall determine by whom such fees shall be borne.

(e) If the dispute, claim, or controversy does not involve, disclose or specify a money claim the non-refundable filing fee will be $250 and the hearing session deposit to be deposited by a party shall be $600, or such greater or lesser amount as the Director of Arbitration or the panel of arbitrators may require, but shall not exceed $1,000.

(f) The Association shall retain the total initial amount deposited as hearing session deposits by all the parties in any matter submitted and settled or withdrawn within eight business days of the first scheduled hearing session other than a prehearing conference.

(g) Any matter submitted and thereafter settled or withdrawn subsequent to the commencement of the first hearing session, including a pre-hearing conference with an arbitrator, shall be subject to an assessment of forum fees and costs incurred pursuant to Sections 30, 32, 33, and 37 based on hearing sessions held and scheduled within eight business days after the Association receives notice that the matter has been settled or withdrawn. The arbitrator(s) shall determine by whom such fees and costs shall be borne.

(h) In each industry or clearing controversy which is required to be submitted to arbitration before the Association as set forth in Section 8, above, requiring expedited hearings, a non-refundable surcharge of $2,500 shall be paid by all Claimants, collectively, and a non-refundable surcharge of $2,500 shall be paid by all Respondents, collectively. These surcharge fees shall be in addition to all other non-refundable filing fees, hearing deposits, or costs which may be required.

Schedule of Fees

Amount in Dispute (Exclusive of Interest and Expenses)	Claim Filing Fee	Hearing Session Deposit		
		Simplified[1]	One Arbitrator[2]	Three Abitrators[3]
$.01–$1,000	$500	$75	$300	NA
$1000.01–$2500	$500	$75	$300	NA
$2,500.01–$5,000	$500	$75	$300	NA
$5,000.01–10,000	$500	$75	$300	NA
$10,000.01–$30,000	$500	NA	$300	$600
$30,000.01–$50,000	$500	NA	$300[4]	$600
$50,000.01–$100,000	$500	NA	$300[4]	$600
$100,000.01–$500,000	$500	NA	$300[4]	$750
$500,000.01–$5,000,000	$500	NA	$300[4]	$1000
Over $5,000,000	$500	NA	$300[4]	$1500

[1]Simplified Arbitration (Without Hearing)

[2]One Arbitrator (Per Hearing Session)
[3]Three or more Arbitrators (Per Hearing Session)
[4]Prehearing Conferences Only
    [Section 45 added effective May 10, 1989; amended effective June
1, 1990.]

- **Selected NASD Notice to Members**
    90--47 Amendments to Code of Arbitration Procedure
                                                        (July 1990)

SECTION SIX

FRANCHISES

A franchise is the purchase of the right to conduct business using certain trademarks that have already been established by a parent company. The parent company, or franchisor, sells the rights to use these trademarks to the individual business owner, or franchisee. Examples of franchises include fast food restaurants, hair salons, home decorating businesses and sports/fitness enterprises.

A franchise may provide the opportunity for an individual who wants to pursue a business with a way to fulfill his or her dreams. But before investing in a franchise, potential franchisees should carefully scrutinize the franchise agreement.

Many franchisors make misrepresentations to potential franchisees regarding their opportunities for earnings or sales. Likewise, misrepresentations may be made with regard to what territory the franchisee will be guaranteed as part of the business, or the success rate that other franchisees have had with similar businesses. In addition, franchisors may tell potential franchisees that they will be independent business owners under the franchise agreement, when in fact the franchise agreement requires the franchisee to adhere to a multitude of franchisor-specified rules and regulations. Finally, the cost of investing in a franchise may be substantial. The more established and well-known the parent company, the greater the investment that will be required of the potential franchisee.

Before investing in any franchise, you should consider factors including:

1. Does the franchise agreement require payment of a certain amount on a monthly or annual basis to the franchisor, regardless of actual profits?

2. Does the franchisor require adherence to certain rules and regulations; if so, does the franchisor impose any penalties for non-adherence? Will such rules and regulations infringe upon your right to conduct business in a manner that you see fit?

3. What arrangements will be made by the franchisor to assist you financially during the start-up time for your franchise? What assistance will the franchisor provide if your franchise goes through "slow" periods? Does the franchisor expect specific returns from the franchise within a specified amount of time?

While franchises are marketed as business opportunities, many franchisors grant franchisees only the rights they would receive as employees, while imposing upon them all of the liabilities associated with being an independent business owner. Franchisors may endeavor to convince individuals to purchase a franchise rather than start their own business by citing the "safety" of the investment in a franchise as opposed to the "risk" of commencing an individually owned business. Potential investors in franchises should carefully investigate such representations, since some studies have shown that franchised businesses actually have a greater risk of failure than businesses that are individually owned.

Before entering into any franchise agreement, obtain all promises that are made by the franchisor in writing. If the franchisor refuses to reduce a representation to writing, this should alert the potential franchisee to the possibility that the franchisor cannot deliver on the promise. Before entering into a franchise agreement, the potential franchisee should have the franchise agreement reviewed by their own legal counsel. Remember, the franchisor is in all probability a large, powerful corporation with hundreds of attorneys at its disposal. The franchisor wants an agreement that best protects its rights and its ability to obtain profits from the franchise. Review of the franchise agreement by the potential franchisee's own lawyer may alert the franchisee to provisions in the agreement that could be potentially detrimental to his or her interests.

If you have purchased a franchise based on misrepresentations that were made by the franchisor, and you believe that you have sustained financial damage as a result, you may wish to consult with an attorney. You should plan to provide your attorney with documentation including all information given to you by the franchisor, the franchise agreement, and financial information for both you and the franchise. As with most claims, you must start your case within the statute of limitations. By consulting with an attorney, you can best protect your rights.

SECTION SEVEN

DISCRIMINATION

Discrimination may occur in many contexts. Individuals have been discriminated against based on classifications including age, gender, gender preference, physical characteristics, skin color, and religious beliefs. Legal action seeking redress for discriminatory acts often arises out of conduct that occurs in the workplace. Examples of potentially actionable claims include:

1. Loss of a deserved promotion or salary increase

2. Employer creates or condones work environment so hostile that employee has no other alternative than to terminate employment

3. Employer engages in specific patterns or practices applicable only to specific groups of employees

4. Career advancement or continued employment conditioned on compliance with employer demands that are unrelated to job duties

Individuals who believe that they have been discriminated against may be able to pursue legal action on a number of grounds. Federal and state law may provide remedies for some claims. In addition, many states permit individuals to bring lawsuits against the person or entity that engaged in the discriminatory conduct.

As in virtually all claims, legal action must be started within a specified amount of time. These time limits vary from state to state. If you believe that you have been injured due to discriminatory conduct, you should seek the advice of an attorney immediately to ensure that your rights are protected.

In order to substantiate a discrimination claim, the injured person should be able to describe the alleged discriminatory conduct with specificity----what was said or done, at what times, in what locations, on how many occasions. Written complaints to supervisory personnel may help to substantiate an injured person's claims. Co-workers may have witnessed or been subjected to the discriminatory conduct, and may thus furnish valuable testimony. Documents such as employee handbooks and company records may likewise provide important information regarding a particular company's approach to handling discriminatory conduct in the workplace. Information pertaining to the job description, educational background, and salary history of the injured person are also important, because they establish what damages have been sustained.

Individuals who have been discriminated against sometimes decline to pursue their legal rights due to fear of further retaliation by their employer or supervisor. But employers are not permitted to take retaliatory action against employees who seek enforcement of their legal rights. Filing a discrimination claim does not ensure that an employee will not be fired or demoted, however. If the employer or supervisor can show a reason for the adverse action that is unrelated to the discrimination claim----for example, poor job performance----the adverse action is unlikely to be regarded as retaliatory.

SECTION EIGHT

DAMAGES

The term "damages" in the context of a legal case ordinarily refers to the total amount of money that will be given to the injured person to make him or her "whole" again after an injury of any kind. Such damages can be divided into two categories----general damages and special damages.

General damages compensate people who have sustained physical or emotional injuries for the past and future pain and suffering associated with those injuries, as well as for any permanent effects associated with those injuries. If you were married at the time of your injury, your spouse may also be entitled to damages for his or her loss of your services due to your injury. General damages are ordinarily established through the testimony of the injured person, the testimony and records of medical care providers, and other expert witnesses. Determining how much to award in general damages is a somewhat subjective process, because every injury is different, and every injured person is affected in a different way.

Special damages reimburse people who have sustained any sort of injury for specific losses that can be documented, such as lost earnings, medical expenses, business losses, and repair bills. Special damages are ordinarily established through documents such as bills, tax returns, canceled checks, payroll records, receipts, and other documents that quantify the value of particular items. Direct testimony of the injured person, the person who provided particular goods or services, and expert economists may also assist in the establishment of special damages.

In addition to general and special damages, which focus on restoring the injured person to the same place where he or she was before the injury, punitive damages are sometimes awarded. The purpose of punitive damages is to punish the defendant, not to make the plaintiff whole again. Punitive damages can only be awarded where the injured person has shown that the defendant's conduct was reckless, malicious, or otherwise in flagrant disregard of the injured person's rights.

If your case is tried in court and it is determined that you are entitled to recover, the jury will award separate amounts to you for your past pain and suffering, future pain and suffering, spouse's claim (if any), lost earnings, out of pocket expenses, and punitive damages (if appropriate). If you settle your case out of court, however, you will probably be offered a lump sum amount, which is intended to encompass all elements of your damages.

SECTION NINE

LAWYERS

SELECTING AND HIRING A LAWYER

Qualifications

When selecting your lawyer, you should consider numerous criteria. First, you should consider whether the lawyer possesses substantial expertise in the type of law involved in your case. You should take into consideration that a lawyer who specializes may be more experienced than a lawyer who practices in all areas of law. A lawyer who specializes deals with cases like yours every working day. Specialized lawyers have a greater awareness of the techniques used by their opponents to slow down and complicate the resolution of cases. Specialized lawyers' relationships with opposing counsel may also be an asset in terms of early resolution of a case by settlement, where appropriate. A lawyer who specializes may have greater trial experience than a general practitioner.

A specialized lawyer will have tried many of the different aspects of cases like yours, whereas a general practitioner may never have tried such a case. A specialized lawyer will also have a greater knowledge of different expert witnesses available to testify in regard to a particular situation, and will have a greater familiarity with the terminology critical to the case. A specialized lawyer will have a clear idea of what to expect with regard to pre-trial discovery procedures. A non-specialized lawyer may do only one or two such proceedings in an entire year, whereas a specialized lawyer handles several of such proceedings in the course of a week. The specialized lawyer will be able to anticipate what questions may be asked of the client, and therefore will better prepare the client to answer such questions. The specialized lawyer will also have a greater understanding of how to handle the extensive paperwork associated with most cases, whereas a general practitioner may not have the time or resources to efficiently process such documents.

Also consider the size of the lawyer's office and what types of resources are available to the office when determining whether a particular lawyer is appropriate for your needs. A lawyer who practices alone may not have the time or financial resources required to handle a particular type of case. On the other hand, a lawyer who works as a team with other lawyers, paralegals and support staff may be able to work more productively on your case, thus offering you better results.

Fees and expenses

When you need a lawyer to help you recover for damages you have sustained due to bodily injuries, investment or business losses, or discriminatory acts, you have two choices. You can hire a lawyer by the hour. Many lawyers charge anywhere from $100.00 to $400.00 per hour. Such costs may be a barrier to hiring a lawyer on an hourly basis.

Your other option is to find a lawyer who works on a contingent fee basis----in other words, a lawyer who charges no legal fee until and unless you win your case. Such arrangements may be preferable to the substantial cost of retaining a lawyer on an hourly basis. In addition, you may feel more confident in a lawyer who invests time and money to fight for your case. It is unlikely that a lawyer would accept a case on a contingent fee basis if he or she does not believe in the case.

When you have your initial meeting with your lawyer, you may wish to have the fee agreement put in writing. By reducing the fee arrangement to writing, both you and your lawyer prevent the chance of a disagreement or misunderstanding later in the case.

The law in most states requires the client to be responsible for all expenses the lawyer incurs to build up the case. Many lawyers charge in advance for expenses they incur in investigating and building a case, which can add up to hundreds or even thousands of dollars. These expenses include the costs of obtaining medical, financial, and employment records, private investigators, expert witnesses, and court costs. Do not be afraid to see a lawyer because the law requires you to be responsible for these expenses. Some law firms will advance all of the money required to build up your case. The money that the lawyer has advanced to build up your case will be deducted from the settlement. Typically, such expenses are small compared to the amount that can be collected on your case.

WHAT IS A RETAINER AGREEMENT?

A retainer agreement is an agreement between the client and the lawyer. This agreement may include information on how much and when the lawyer will be paid, as well as when and who will pay for the expenses associated with investigation and litigation of the case. Most agreements in cases seeking to recover for personal or financial injuries call for the lawyer to collect a fee only if the case is settled or won in court. A percentage of the amount settled for or won is paid to the lawyer. The agreement may also provide for what happens if the client decides to change lawyers. Further, a retainer agreement may contain the client's authorization for the law firm to investigate the claim, and may permit the lawyer to stop working on the case if the lawyer discovers that there is no valid claim.

The agreement is required by law in some states. In other states, such agreements are optional. It is good business, however, for both the lawyer and client to insist on a written agreement.

YOUR RELATIONSHIP WITH YOUR LAWYER

Your relationship with your lawyer is confidential. Communications between you and your lawyer are ordinarily private and privileged. This means that your lawyer cannot reveal information that you tell him or her without your consent.

The lawyer you retain should be someone you can trust. In order to best serve you, your lawyer needs to know everything about your case, even details that are embarrassing or potentially damaging to your case.

If you do not have the utmost of faith in a lawyer's abilities, then you should not be represented by that lawyer. In the course of settling or litigating a claim, your lawyer will give you advice which your lawyer will offer with your best interests in mind. If you feel that you cannot trust your lawyer, then you will not trust your lawyer's advice. This situation can be avoided if you carefully consider your feelings when choosing your lawyer.

A lawyer is obligated to represent each and every client to the best of his or her abilities. As a professional, your lawyer should take pride in the representation that he or she offers. Further, your lawyer should be responsive to your needs regarding your case.

Your lawyer is an advocate for your claim. It is unlikely that he or she will cheat you, particularly if the lawyer represents many people with claims like yours. If such a lawyer cheated just one client, the lawyer's reputation could be ruined. A lawyer foolish enough to accept a "payoff" from the other side could lose his or her license to practice law. It is unlikely that a lawyer would risk his or her career for just one case.

While it is preferable to find a lawyer with whom you are comfortable at the start, and stay with that lawyer throughout your case, circumstances may arise under which you may elect to change attorneys. Under such circumstances, your original lawyer will be entitled to compensation for the work he or she performed on your case. This money must be paid out of the attorney's fee that your new lawyer collects when the case reaches judgment or settlement, unless you already made payment arrangements with your original lawyer.

Transferring a case from one lawyer to another can be a time-consuming process. Sometimes the lawyers will argue about the what share of the fee each should receive. Your new lawyer may require time to review and understand your case. Such matters may slow down the resolution of your case.

CAN YOUR LAWYER GIVE YOU A CASH ADVANCE?

Even though your lawyer may want to assist you in putting your life back together after a personal injury or a financial loss, he or she is legally forbidden from providing such help in the form of a cash advance on the proceeds of your settlement. One reason underlying this prohibition is that if a lawyer advanced you cash from your settlement, the lawyer might advise you to settle early, considering his or her own self-interest above your welfare.

The law sets strict ethical guidelines that govern relations between attorneys and their clients. If your lawyer violates these standards, he or she could be barred or suspended from practicing law. No reputable lawyer would risk his or her career for the sake of one client. Therefore, a lawyer's willingness to give you a cash advance on your settlement should alert you to the possibility that the lawyer is not serving your best interests.

HOW TO BE A GOOD CLIENT

You can help your lawyer in many ways:

1. Retain a lawyer experienced with your type of case.

2. Keep all scheduled appointments. If you wish to speak with the lawyer in person, call to make an appointment. Do not go to the lawyer's office without an appointment.

3. Keep detailed notes of your problems and questions so that you can review them with your lawyer.

4. Do not ask a lawyer to give a cash advance.

5. Give your lawyer a reasonable time to return your phone calls. Lawyers are often out of their offices, and thus are not always available to return phone calls immediately.

6. Be completely honest with your lawyer. Tell your lawyer everything about your claim, no matter how insignificant or embarrassing. If you lie to your lawyer or do not tell your lawyer about a potential problem with your case, your lawyer will be at a disadvantage if the problem comes up. Lawyers are used to problems and can work with you to overcome them as long as they know about the problems in advance.

7. Promptly respond to any requests your lawyer makes. For example, if your lawyer asks for copies of your medical bills, he or she has a reason for doing so, and that reason relates to your case. By quickly giving your lawyer the information he or she asks for, you can help to advance your case.

8. Tell the lawyer if you are unhappy. Lawyers need clients, and want to keep them satisfied. If you are unhappy, your lawyer needs to know why so that he or she can better serve you.

9. Remember that your lawyer wants to get the largest possible amount that is fair to compensate you. Sometimes this can take a long time. Your lawyer will appreciate your patience while he or she is working to get you the maximum amount possible.

QUESTIONS YOUR LAWYER WILL ASK

When you first meet with your lawyer, you will be asked many questions. These are aimed at getting the information needed to investigate and prepare your claim. Your attorney can not afford to be surprised later about an important piece of information. The following is a list of common questions asked by lawyers of their clients:

1. Name

2. Home address

3. Phone number

4. Age

5. Social Security Number

6. Marital status

7. Spouse's name

8. Age of spouse

9. Children's names and ages

10. Work address

11. Work phone number

12. Other phone numbers to reach you

13. List of all persons living in household and ages and if they are dependent on you

14. Names of any individuals, including representatives of the defendant or its insurance company, with whom you have already discussed your claim.

15. Copies of any documents that are pertinent to your claim.

16. Describe the state of your health and your financial circumstances prior to the events giving rise to your claim.

17. Provide information about your job title, duties performed, rate of pay, and hours worked prior to the incident giving rise to your claim.

18. Provide documentation of any loss of earnings that you are seeking to recover.

19. Name any witnesses to events pertinent to your claim.

20. Describe any physical problems that have arisen due to your claim.

21. Describe any collateral sources that you have received for—example, workers' compensation, unemployment compensation, no-fault benefits, disability insurance, and welfare benefits all constitute collateral sources.

22. List all expenses that you believe have been incurred as a result of your claim.

23. List all experts with whom you have consulted—such as doctors, economists, accountants, etc.

SECTION TEN

WHAT IS INVOLVED IN THE CLAIMS PROCESS?

CLAIMS ADJUSTERS

After an accident or injury occurs, a representative of the other side may contact you. This representative is generally a claims adjuster for an insurance company. The adjuster's job is to investigate the circumstances surrounding your injury. The adjuster's objective is to minimize the amount of money that the insurance company will have to pay to settle the case. Once the case is settled, it can never be reopened. Therefore, the adjuster wants to settle the case quickly, and for the smallest amount of money possible.

Insurance adjusters also locate witnesses, obtain photographs of accident scenes, and obtain reports filed by police or other agencies. The adjuster may also seek to obtain information about the medical treatment that you have undergone. With this information, the adjuster will evaluate the claim and arrive at an amount that he or she is willing to offer to you in settlement of your claim.

In cases where injuries have been sustained as a result of accidents, the adjuster will frequently call shortly after the accident. The adjuster may offer to come to your home or hospital room to discuss the claim. The adjuster may express concern for your situation, and offer to provide money to assist you with your immediate needs.

You should beware of dealing with adjusters under these circumstances. The adjuster may take advantage of your vulnerability following an injury in order to achieve his or her goal of a fast settlement for a minimal amount of money.

STATEMENTS

The insurance adjuster may also seek to visit your home or hospital room to obtain your statement about the accident. The adjuster may also contact you by telephone in an effort to obtain such a statement.

Individuals who have sustained injuries are often confused about what information they are required to provide in order to protect their rights. The insurance adjuster may try to take advantage of such confusion. For example, the adjuster may say that your claim cannot be processed without your statement.

If you have been injured in an accident, you are not required to speak with the insurance adjuster who represents the other side. You must report the accident to your own insurance company and provide your own insurance company with a statement of the facts. You have no obligation to assist the other side's insurance company in developing its case.

If you have already given a statement to an insurance adjuster----whether from your own insurance company or from the insurance company for the other side----you are entitled to receive a copy of this statement. If the adjuster fails to provide a copy to you, you should request a copy in writing from the adjuster. Such statements are important because they reflect your perceptions of an accident immediately after it occurred, when details such as weather and roadway conditions, vehicle locations, witnesses, and actions taken by all parties involved are fresh in your mind. Further, such statements are often important, because they are given at a time when the people involved in the accident have not yet had an opportunity to reflect on the facts of the accident with self-interest in mind.

MEDICAL AUTHORIZATIONS

If you have been injured, there is nothing that you can do to prevent an insurance adjuster from speaking with witnesses, police officers, and other individuals who might have knowledge about the incident that caused your injuries. Likewise, there is nothing that you can do to prevent the adjuster from obtaining documents such as police reports which are public records. There is one source of information, however, that you can control. This source is your medical records.

The adjuster may ask you to sign an authorization form allowing him or her to obtain copies of your medical records. It is highly inadvisable to sign such a form without seeking legal advice. Adjusters will generally seek a very broad authorization. A broadly worded authorization will allow the adjuster to inquire into any and all of your medical records, including those that existed prior to the injury giving rise to your claim. If you sign such an authorization, the adjuster will be able to browse freely among all of your medical records, even if they bear no relationship to your claim. The adjuster may then use any information obtained through such records in an effort to try and minimize the value of your case. For example, if you injure your knee in a motor vehicle accident and subsequently give the adjuster an unlimited medical authorization, the adjuster might look in your medical records and find that you had injured the same knee several years ago. The adjuster might then argue that your injuries are related to your previous injury, rather than to the accident from which your present claim arises.

SETTLEMENT OFFERS

The adjuster may elect to offer you a settlement. If you are not represented by an attorney, it is unlikely that you will know whether the adjuster's offer is fair. If you settle a case without seeking legal advice, you may be cheating yourself out of thousands of dollars. The adjuster is highly experienced in handling claims such as yours, whereas you have probably never been involved in such a matter before. By consulting an attorney who is experienced in handling cases such as yours, you can help to put yourself on an even footing with the adjuster, and work toward a settlement which fairly reflects the value of your case.

Once you have hired an attorney, the attorney will gather information about your case. Much of the information that your attorney gathers will be the same type of information that the adjuster obtains----witness statements, police reports, photographs, and medical records. Your attorney may provide the adjuster with information that will enable the adjuster to evaluate your claim, but will probably restrict the adjuster's access to other records.

Once your doctors have concluded that you have reached a point of maximum improvement from your injuries, your attorney may endeavor to settle your claim. Your attorney may prepare a demand letter or settlement package to send to the adjuster. Information contained in a demand letter or settlement package might include a summary of the accident and the injuries that you sustained, medical records documenting your treatment history and the permanent effects associated with your injuries, medical bills, photographs of your injuries and/or of the accident scene, and any other information that your attorney believes is important to your case. Your attorney may also specify an amount of money that he or she believes would be appropriate to settle your case. Such settlement demands generally provide the insurance company with a time frame in which to respond with a settlement offer; if settlement negotiations are not initiated within that time, the attorney may start a lawsuit to show the insurance company that he or she is serious about obtaining a fair amount for your injuries.

The insurance company may respond to your attorney's settlement demand. It is unlikely, however, that the attorney's demand will be met. It is much more likely that the insurance company will make a counteroffer, and the process of negotiating between your attorney and the insurance company will begin. On some occasions, both sides will be able to reach a compromise that reflects a fair value for your case. In other instances, however, the insurance company will refuse, even after extended negotiations, to offer a fair settlement. In such instances, the attorney will have no alternative but to initiate a lawsuit to further pursue your claim.

RELEASES

In the event that a mutually satisfactory settlement is reached, your attorney will provide you with a release form to sign. Releases ordinarily provide that in exchange for a particular sum of money, the injured person ends any and all claims that he or she may have against the person who is responsible for causing his or her injuries. Signing a release means that you are ending your case. Once you have signed a release and given it to the insurance company, you cannot change your mind and decide that you want more money. Even if you discover that your injuries are much more serious than you thought, you cannot re-open the case in an effort to recover more money.

INSURANCE COMPANY BAD FAITH

On occasion, the facts surrounding a case will clearly demonstrate the injured person's entitlement to a substantial recovery. If the amount of insurance coverage available is far less than the value of the injuries, the insurance company has an obligation to quickly resolve the claim by payment of the full policy limits. If the insurance company fails to do so, such failure may be regarded as bad faith. If the insurance company is found to be in bad faith, the insurance company may be required to pay the injured person over and about its policy limits. If your attorney believes that the insurance company is acting in bad faith with regard to its refusal to settle your claim, he or she will take the necessary steps to preserve your rights to recover directly against the insurance company.

WHERE TO COMPLAIN ABOUT INSURANCE COMPANIES

ALABAMA:	Alabama Insurance Department; 135 South Union Street; Montgomery, AL 36130-3401; 205/269-3550
ALASKA:	Alaska Insurance Department; 800 East Diamond, Suite 560; Anchorage, AK 99515; 907/349-1230
ARIZONA:	Arizona Insurance Department; Consumer Affairs and Investigation; 3030 North Third Street; Phoenix, AZ 85012; 602/255-4783
ARKANSAS:	Arkansas Insurance Department; Consumer Service Division; 400 University Tower Building; 12th and University Streets; Little Rock, AR 72204; 501/686-2945
CALIFORNIA:	California Insurance Department; Consumer Services Division; Claims Service Bureau; 3450 Wilshire Boulevard; Los Angeles, CA 90010; 800/927-4357 (within state)
COLORADO:	Colorado Insurance Division; 1560 Broadway, Suite 850; Denver, CO 80202; 303/894-7499
CONNECTICUT:	Connecticut Insurance Department; Post Office Box 816; Hartford, CT 06142-0816; 203/297-3800
DELAWARE:	Delaware Insurance Department; 841 Silver Lake Boulevard; Dover, DE 19901; 302/739-4251

DISTRICT OF COLUMBIA:	District of Columbia Insurance Department; 613 G Street, NW Room 619; Post Office Box 37200; Washington, DC 20013-7200; 202/727-8017
FLORIDA:	Florida Department of Insurance; State Capitol; Plaza Level Eleven; 200 East Gaines Street; Tallahassee, FL 32399-0300; 800/342-2762 (within state); 904/922-3100
GEORGIA:	Georgia Insurance Department; 2 Martin Luther King, Jr. Drive; Room 716, West Tower; Atlanta, GA 30334; 404/656-2056
HAWAII:	Hawaii Department of Commerce and Consumer Affairs; Insurance Division; Post Office Box 3614; Honolulu, HI 96811-3614; 808/586-2790
IDAHO:	Idaho Insurance Department; Public Service Department; 500 South 10th Street; Boise, ID 83720; 208/334-4250
ILLINOIS:	Illinois Insurance Department; 320 West Washington Street, 4th Floor; Springfield, IL 62767; 217/782-4515
INDIANA:	Indiana Insurance Department; 311 West Washington Street, Suite 300; Indianapolis, IN 46204; 317/232-2395
IOWA:	Iowa Insurance Division; Lucas State Office Building; East 12th and Grand Streets; Des Moines, IA 50319; 515/281-5705
KANSAS:	Kansas Insurance Department; 420 Southwest 9th Street; Topeka, KS 66612-1678; 913/296-3071

KENTUCKY:	Kentucky Insurance Department; 229 West Main Street; Post Office Box 517; Frankfort, KY 40602; 502/564-3630
LOUISIANA:	Louisiana Insurance Department; Post Office Box 94214; Baton Rouge, LA 70804-9214; 504/342-5900
MAINE:	Maine Bureau of insurance; Consumer Division; State House, Station #34; Augusta, ME 04333; 207/582-8707
MARYLAND:	Maryland Insurance Department; Complaints and Investigation Unit; 501 St. Paul Place; Baltimore, MD 21202-2272; 410/333-6300
MASSACHUSETTS:	Massachusetts Insurance Division; Consumer Services Section; 280 Friend Street; Boston, MA 02114; 617/727-7189
MICHIGAN:	Michigan Insurance Department; Post Office Box 30220; Lansing, MI 48909; 517/373-0220
MINNESOTA:	Minnesota Insurance Department; Department of Commerce; 133 East 7th Street; St. Paul, MN 55101; 612/296-4026
MISSISSIPPI:	Mississippi Insurance Department; Consumer Assistance Division; Post Office Box 79; Jackson, MS 39205; 601/359-3569
MISSOURI:	Missouri Division of Insurance; Consumer Services Section; Post Office Box 690; Jefferson City, MO 65102-0690; 314/751-2640
MONTANA:	Montana Insurance Department; 126 North Sanders, Room 270; Post Office

	Box 4009; Helena, MT 59604; 800/332-6148 (within state); 406/444-2040
NEBRASKA:	Nebraska Insurance Department; Terminal Building; 941 0 Street, Suite 400; Lincoln, NE 68508; 402/471-2201
NEVADA:	Nevada Department of Commerce; Insurance Division, Consumer Section; 1665 Hot Springs Road; Capitol Complex, Suite 152; Carson City, NV 89701; 702/687-4270
NEW HAMPSHIRE:	New Hampshire Insurance Department; Life and Health Division; 169 Manchester Street; Concord, NH 03301-5151; 603/271-2261
NEW JERSEY:	New Jersey Insurance Department; 20 West State Street; Roebling Building; Trenton, NJ 08625-0325; 609/292-4757
NEW MEXICO:	New Mexico Insurance Department; Post Office Drawer 1269; Santa Fe, NM 87504-1269; 505/827-4500
NEW YORK:	New York Insurance Department; 160 West Broadway; New York, NY 10013; 212/602-0203 (New York City); 800/342-3736 (within state, outside NYC)
NORTH CAROLINA:	North Carolina Insurance Department; Consumer Services; Post Office Box 26387; Raleigh, NC 27611; 919/733-2004
NORTH DAKOTA:	North Dakota Insurance Department; Capitol Building, 5th Floor; 600 East Boulevard Avenue; Bismarck, ND 58505-0320; 701/224-2440

OHIO:	Ohio Insurance Department; Consumer Services Division; 2100 Stella Court; Columbus, OH 43266-0566; 614/644-2673
OKLAHOMA:	Oklahoma Insurance Department; Post Office Box 53408; Oklahoma City, OK 73152-3408; 405/521-2828
OREGON:	Oregon Department of Insurance and Finance; Insurance Division/Consumer Advocate; 440-7 Labor and Industry Building; Salem, OR 97310; 503/378-4484
PENNSYLVANIA:	Pennsylvania Insurance Department; 1321 Strawberry Square; Harrisburg, PA 17120; 717/787-2317
RHODE ISLAND:	Rhode Island Insurance Division; 233 Richmond Street, Suite 233; Providence, RI 02903-4233; 401/277-2223
SOUTH CAROLINA:	South Carolina Insurance Department; Post Office Box 100105; Columbia, SC 29202-3105; 803/737-6140
SOUTH DAKOTA:	South Dakota Insurance Department; Consumer Assistance Section; 500 East Central; Pierre, SD 57501-3940; 605/773-3563
TENNESSEE:	Tennessee Department of Commerce and Insurance; Policyholders Service Section; 500 James Robertson Parkway, 4th Floor; Nashville, TN 37243-0582; 800/342-4029 (within state); 615/741-4955
TEXAS:	Texas Board of Insurance Complaints Division; 1110 San Jacinto Boulevard; Austin, TX 78701-1998; 512/463-6501

UTAH:	Utah Insurance Department; Consumer Services; 3110 State Office Building; Salt Lake City, UT 84114; 801/530-6400
VERMONT:	Vermont Department of Insurance and Banking; Consumer Complaint Division; 120 State Street; Montpelier, VT 05602; 802/828-3301
VIRGINIA:	Virginia Insurance Department; Consumer Services Division; 700 Jefferson Building; Post Office Box 1157; Richmond, VA 23209; 804/786-7691
WASHINGTON:	Washington Insurance Department; Insurance Building; Post Office Box 40255; Olympia, WA 98504-0255; 800/562-6900 (within state); 206/753-7300
WEST VIRGINIA:	West Virginia Insurance Department; Post Office Box 50540; 2019 Washington Street, East; Charleston, WV 25305-0540; 304/558-3386
WISCONSIN:	Wisconsin Insurance Department; Complaints Department; Post Office Box 7873; Madison, WI 53707; 608/266-0103
WYOMING:	Wyoming Insurance Department; Herschler Building; 122 West 25th Street; Cheyenne, WY 82002; 307/777-7401

SECTION ELEVEN

CONSIDERATIONS BEFORE SETTLING ANY CLAIM

HOW MUCH IS YOUR CASE WORTH

The most frequently asked question before a case is won or settled is, "How much is my case worth?" When you first see a lawyer, it is difficult to answer this question. Without development of the pertinent facts surrounding the case, even a "ballpark" figure cannot be stated. In many cases, only a jury can decide how much money you will ultimately receive. Your lawyer needs to know the answers to many questions before giving you an idea of the value of your case. Examples of these questions are listed below:

Questions that apply to all cases:

1. Are you willing to go to court to fight your case?

2. Do you have witnesses who support your claim?

3. Does the opposing party or insurance company prefer to settle or go to court?

4. Will you make a sympathetic witness in court?

5. Is your lawyer known as an experienced lawyer who will fight in court, if needed?

6. How long will it take to schedule a trial in court?

7. How much will it cost to go to court (consider expert witness fees, court costs, and the "time value of money")?

8. How much have juries awarded in the past to other people who have brought cases such as yours?

Questions that apply to cases involving bodily injuries:

1. How did your injuries occur?

2. What kind of injuries did you sustain?

3. Will you need future medical care?

4. Have you followed your doctor's orders for treatment?

5. Did you have any pre-existing injuries or health problems?

6. Did you cause or aggravate your own injuries?

7. Have you sustained any out-of-pocket expenses (such as medical bills, prescriptions, nursing services not covered by insurance) due to your injuries?

8. Have you lost money due to missing time from work?

9. Does your doctor expect your injuries to be permanent?

If your injuries were sustained due to an accident, you should also ask:

10. How did the accident occur?

11. Who was at fault for the accident?

12. Was the accident reported to the police or other authorities?

13. Did you contribute to the accident by violating any laws? For example, in a motor vehicle accident, were you speeding?

If your accident involved a condition that you claim was defective----such as an icy area or a malfunctioning product----you should also ask:

14. Did the person responsible for maintaining the dangerous area or defective product know or have reason

to know that a problem existed <u>before</u> your accident occurred?

Questions that apply to cases involving business or investment losses:

1. What was your financial situation prior to making the transaction that caused your loss?

2. What did you do to investigate the transaction before investing your funds? Was the stockbroker or franchisor your only source of information?

3. Did the stockbroker or franchisor misrepresent any important facts, or make promises that were not delivered?

4. How much money did you invest?

5. How much money did you lose?

If your claim arises out of a transaction involving stock or other securities, you should also ask:

6. Was the investment a suitable one for the broker to sell to you?

7. Did the broker encourage you to make frequent, unnecessary trades?

8. Did the broker make unauthorized trades?

Questions that apply to cases involving discrimination:

1. Did the person or entity that committed the discriminatory act give a justification or pretext for doing so? For example, were "safety reasons" cited to prevent women from obtaining certain jobs?

2. Does the discriminatory person or entity have a history of engaging in similar conduct toward others?

3. Was the discriminatory conduct reported to anyone else at the time that it occurred?

4. What financial losses have you suffered as a result of the discriminatory conduct?

If the discriminatory conduct occurred in your workplace, you should also ask:

5. What sort of work performance did you have prior to being confronted with the discriminatory conduct? Could any aspect of your prior work performance be used as a pretext for such conduct?

Someone who has had a similar case may try to tell you that your claim is worth a certain amount. Such advice is rarely accurate. Since every case and every individual are unique, it is impossible to say that a value that was fair for one person would be fair when applied to someone else. For example, the other person may not have the same severity of an injury as you. It is reasonable to assume that someone with a permanent injury, causing them pain and suffering for the rest of their life, will collect more cash and benefits than a person who has made a complete recovery.

Your lawyer will fight for you with the responsible party or insurance company. Your lawyer will negotiate with the other side to receive their highest offer to settle your case without going to court. Your lawyer will then explain to you the arguments in favor of your case and the opposing side's arguments against your case. Then your lawyer will advise you of his or her opinion concerning the value of your case. You will know how much the other side believes your case to be worth from the settlement offer. You will also have your lawyer's opinion. You can then make your choice to go to trial or to settle out of court.

Remember, no lawyer can tell you how much your case is worth to the penny. If your case is not settled out of court, a jury or judge will decide how much you will receive. The facts of every case are different. Similar cases may have different outcomes. You may receive much more money than you anticipated. In some cases, you might discover that you are entitled to receive less than you thought. More than 90% of all civil cases are settled out of court or before a trial is complete. This is because both sides are apprehensive of the unknown outcome of a trial.

HOW LONG DOES IT TAKE TO RECOVER
MONEY ON A CASE

An important factor in determining whether to settle a case or wait for a trial in court is your recovery time. In general, you will receive money at an earlier date if you elect to accept a settlement offer rather than proceed to trial. You can only win or settle a case once. If the case is settled before you realize the full extent of your injuries, it will be too late to go back and recover for these losses.

After you and your lawyer have gathered information about the extent of your injuries or losses, resolution of your claim can take anywhere from a few months to several years. The length of time involved depends on factors including the nature and extent of your injuries or losses; the situation that gives rise to your claim; the evidence that your lawyer can present in support of your position; and the evidence that the other side may possess in opposition to your case.

In some cases, a fair offer to settle will not be made until you pick a jury at your trial. On occasion, no offer to settle will be ever be extended, and you must rely on the jury to decide the value of your case.

SHOULD YOU GO TO COURT OR SETTLE?

With most claims, a time will come when the other side will make an offer to settle your case without going to court. You will then need to decide whether to accept the settlement or wait for a trial.

The advantages of settling your case out of court include the following:

1. You know how much you will receive.

2. You will receive your money now rather than later.

3. You have no risk of losing and getting nothing for your injuries.

4. You will not have to undergo cross-examination in court by the lawyer for the other side.

5. You will not have to pay additional court costs, expert witness fees, and further investigation costs.

6. You will not be surprised by new information that could hurt or ruin your claim.

7. You can put the matter behind you and go on with your life.

8. You will not risk the chance that the defendant or its insurance company will go bankrupt before you win. It is useless to win if you cannot collect.

The disadvantages of settling your case include the following:

1. You can only win or settle one time. You cannot go back and ask for more money if you later find out that you have sustained additional damages, or if your

damages become more serious than they currently appear.

2. A jury could give much more money than the current settlement offer.

3. You will not have your "day in court."

4. You might find new information that adds value to your case.

Most cases settle out of court. This is because the lawyers for both sides know that juries can give a large award, a small award, or no award at all. Trials are expensive for both sides. A lawyer's time in court is worth thousands of dollars each day. Expert witnesses' fees can be immense. The total cost of going to court, combined with the unknown outcome, often makes the decision easy.

In some cases, however, the other side makes an offer that is not fair. Going to court makes sense in these instances. A small offer means little risk to your case.

You should consult with your lawyer and ask his or her advice on settling any claim. Law firms that handle claims such as yours will know the tactics used by the other side, and will know whether a settlement offer is fair.

Lawyers should be willing to go to court when they believe that an offer is unfair. The other side will take advantage of any lawyer who is afraid of court. A good lawyer will fight in court for his or her client's rights and money whenever necessary.

WHAT ARE LIENS AND HOW DO THEY AFFECT SETTLEMENT OF A CASE?

During the course of working on an injured person's claim, a lawyer may become aware of bills that the client owes, such as for medical treatment associated with the client's injuries. If there is no insurance coverage available to pay these bills, and if the client is unable to pay them out of his or her own pocket, the attorney may make arrangements for a lien to be placed against the settlement proceeds. The lien reflects the financial interest of someone else, in this example, a medical care provider, in the settlement proceeds. The amount of the lien will be deducted from the injured person's proceeds before the injured person receives any money. In this example, the lien may be of benefit to the injured person by keeping the unpaid medical bills out of collection, and assuring the medical care providers that their bills will be paid upon settlement of the case.

Another situation where liens can arise is where the injured person has both a Workers' Compensation claim and an action for personal injuries (third party action). When the third party action is settled, the insurance company that provided Workers' Compensation will expect to be reimbursed from the settlement proceeds for any amounts that it has paid for medical expenses and lost earnings. This expectation of repayment is reflected as a lien against the injured person's settlement proceeds.

One exception to the rule that workers compensation be repaid is where the worker's injury arises our of a motor vehicle accident. In that case, workers' compensation is paying the same benefits that no-fault insurance would ordinarily pay (lost earnings and medical expenses). Since no-fault benefits do not have to be repaid upon settlement, workers compensation benefits that are paid to worker for injuries sustained in a motor vehicle accident do not have to be repaid. In the event that workers' compensation paid out more benefits than no-fault would have given, there may be a lien, but the lien will be limited to the difference between what workers' compensation actually paid and what no-fault would have paid.

Liens may also be asserted by agencies that provide welfare benefits if the injured person has received such benefits associated with their injuries. Likewise, if the injured person has received benefits through their own private insurance, the private insurance company may also assert a lien on the settlement proceeds.

In some instances, the amount of the lien may be so high that it prevents a reasonable settlement from being reached. Under such circumstances, the attorney for the injured person may endeavor to negotiate a reduction of the lien. Lienholders frequently consent to such reductions, since they recognize that they may receive no money at all if the case proceeds to trial. By compromising, the lienholders will receive some money, which they may regard as a more attractive option than being faced with the risk of receiving no money at all.

ARE THERE TAXES ON SETTLEMENTS?

When you sustain a bodily injury, you often have medical bills, lost earnings, and pain and suffering. You would not have incurred any of these losses if your injury never occurred. Investment or business losses are often losses of money that the investor has saved over the course of many years. Discrimination cases often compensate the claimant for money that he or she could have earned, but for the discriminatory conduct.

Settlements and awards are intended to reimburse you for your losses; to make you whole again. You are not "ahead of the game" because of your case. For this reason, Congress has exempted most settlements and awards from tax. When you win your case, you probably will not pay taxes on the proceeds of your verdict or settlement.

SETTLEMENT CHECKLIST

You can only settle or win a case once. After your case has been settled or tried in court, you cannot go back and ask for more money, even if you find out that your damages are worse than you thought, or if new damages arise. Therefore, you should carefully consider the following:

1. What are the advantages of settling out of court?

2. Will I collect more or less if I go to court?

3. How long will I wait for my money if my case goes to court?

4. How much will I get after paying the lawyer?

5. When will I be paid?

6. Who will pay, and where does the money come from?

7. Are there additional parties against whom the claim should be asserted?

8. Are there any additional sources of settlement monies— for example, umbrella coverage, underinsurance coverage?

9. What benefits do I have in addition to my settlement (collateral sources)—for example, no-fault insurance, workers compensation, unemployment compensation, disability benefits?

10. Who pays for future medical bills?

11. Do I have to repay any liens or collateral sources?

12. Is there tax on the settlement amount?

13. What do my expert witnesses—for example, doctors, economists, accountants—say about my injuries?

14. What does my lawyer recommend?

15. If I am married, does my spouse have to agree to settle?

SECTION TWELVE

STATUTES OF LIMITATION

Statutes of limitations are time deadlines which are set by state law, and are applicable to virtually all legal claims. If you fail to bring a lawsuit on your claim within the appropriate statute of limitations, the claim will be barred forever, regardless of the seriousness of your injuries. Since statutes of limitations vary from state to state, and also differ based on the type of case that is being asserted, it is important to seek legal advice as soon as you are aware that you have been injured. By consulting with a lawyer, you will learn the applicable statute of limitations for your case.

The statute of limitations ordinarily begins to run on the date that an injury occurs, but certain conditions can extend the otherwise-applicable statute of limitations. Examples of events that might extend a statute of limitations include:

1. If an injury was not immediately susceptible to discovery—for example, if you underwent surgery and the doctor left a surgical instrument inside of you, you might not immediately discover that you had been injured. Your statute of limitations would probably begin to run from the date that you discovered that the implement had been left inside of you, not from the date of your surgery.

2. If the injured person was under the age of majority at the time that the injury occurred—for example, your child sustained a personal injury at age 11, and you elected to take no action with regard to pursuing a claim. The statute of limitations would be suspended (tolled) until your child reached the age of majority. Once your child reached the age of majority, he or she would be required to bring a claim on his or her own behalf within a specified amount of time.

3. If the injured person was not competent to bring action on his or her own behalf, the statute of limitations

would likewise be suspended or tolled during the period of disability.

Learning the correct statute of limitations that applies to your case is one of the most critical factors toward insuring recovery on your claim. Therefore, you should immediately seek legal counsel once you learn of your injury to clarify which statute of limitations applies.

SECTION THIRTEEN

CLAIMS AGAINST GOVERNMENT BODIES

Many cases involve claims against government bodies, whether at the federal, state or local level. Examples of such claims include:

1. If the government was the owner of a vehicle involved in an accident;

2. If an accident occurred on government property;

3. If a roadway maintained by a government body was defectively designed or maintained, thereby causing an accident.

If you believe that you have a claim against a government body, it is critical that you immediately seek legal advice. Virtually all government bodies require that injured persons notify the government body of the existence of their claim within a specified amount of time. This time limit is often very short, requiring filing within a matter of weeks after the incident giving rise to the claim. Failure to file such notification may prevent the injured person from ever recovering for their injuries.

This filing of a notice of the claim is separate from the requirement that a lawsuit be filed within the statute of limitations. As in all cases, lawsuits against government bodies must be filed within specific time deadlines. The timely filing of a notice of claim does not relieve the injured person of the obligation to start a lawsuit within the statute of limitations. Statutes of limitations against government bodies are also often shorter than statutes of limitations that apply to similar cases involving non-government defendants.

SECTION FOURTEEN

WORKERS' COMPENSATION CLAIMS

INTRODUCTION

If you are injured while you are on the job, Workers' Compensation will generally pay for your medical expenses and some portion of your lost wages. When you recover Workers' Compensation, you are not able to sue your employer. In some cases, however, you might sustain an injury on the job as a result of the conduct of somebody other than your employer. In such a case, even though you are entitled to collect Workers' Compensation, you might be able to bring an action against that other party. For example, if you were on the job using a machine that did not have proper safety devices, and you were hurt as a result, you could recover from Workers' Compensation **and** you could bring an action against the manufacturer and seller of the machine. Likewise, if you were driving a motor vehicle as part of your job, and you were involved in an accident and were injured, you could collect Workers' Compensation **and** you could sue the driver of the other vehicle. Cases such as these are called "third-party claims" because you are suing a third party other than your employer.

In such cases, Workers' Compensation will have what is called a lien on the proceeds that you receive from the third-party action. This means that Workers' Compensation will already have paid you for some of the same damages that you will recover from the third-party action (for example, lost wages and medical expenses). While you will repay Workers' Compensation for this lien, you can also receive additional money for the third-party action that you do not have to pay back.

THINGS TO DO IF YOU ARE HURT ON THE JOB

1. Seek medical attention. Advise your doctor of all your problems and that the accident occurred while at work. Follow your doctor's instructions for medical care.

2. Report the accident to your employer or supervisor and make sure that your employer takes a written report.

3. Get the name of your employer's workers compensation insurance carrier.

4. Obtain the names of all witnesses, along with their addresses and phone numbers.

5. Ask your doctor for a written statement of how long you should stay out of work.

6. If you were injured while using a piece of machinery, obtain the manufacturer's name, serial numbers, and any other information available about the machine. Take photographs of the machine, if possible.

7. Consult a personal injury lawyer to determine your legal rights with regard to claims for workers compensation and/or against any third party.

ABOUT THE AUTHOR

James J. Shapiro is a founder of the law firm of Shapiro & Shapiro, and is a member of the American Trial Lawyers Association and The Plaintiffs Securities Lawyers Group "PI-ABA". He graduated from the Boston University Law School Masters Program, is a member of the Florida, New York and Pennsylvania Bar Associations, and president of James J. Shapiro, P.A.

Mr. Shapiro started the law firm Shapiro & Shapiro with his father, Sidney Shapiro. James Shapiro has law offices in Dade and Broward Counties in Florida, as well as offices in Rochester, Syracuse and Buffalo, New York.

Mr. Shapiro has helped thousands of people by answering questions and telling the secrets used by insurance companies, corporations, and other defendants. He has been interviewed on radio talk shows across the country including the well-known program "Your Personal Finance", as well as on stations WEBT in New York City; WBVB and KDKA in Pittsburgh; WBZT in Palm Beach, Florida; WLIP in Kenosha, Wisconsin; KCED in San Diego/Carlsbad. As a result of Mr. Shapiro's frequent talk show broadcasts, listeners have created such a demand for his first book "INJURY VICTIMS RIGHTS TO MAXIMUM CASH" that over 20,000 copies are now in print.

James Shapiro is a tough, smart, aggressive lawyer who has made a lifetime commitment to helping victims win cash awards.

FREE UPDATES AND QUESTIONS:

If you have questions about this book...

If you would like free updates to this book...

If you would like to receive a free newsletter...

Contact **James Shapiro** at **1-800-3456-LAW**
(1-800-345-6529)

QUESTIONS

To receive the answers to your personal questions, please send your questions to the address below. We will attempt to answer your questions at no charge in our next newsletter or revised editions of this book.

To obtain free updates and newsletters, simply send your name and address to:

James Shapiro
Maximum Cash Book
1820 First Federal Plaza
Rochester, New York 14614

or phone 1–800–345–6LAW
(1–800–345–6529).

NOTES